John Thaw 1942–2002:
An Appreciation

Edited by Susan Elkin

John Thaw
1942–2002:
An Appreciation

Edited by Susan Elkin

elius
books

Liverpool England

First published in the United Kingdom 2002
by DV Knox-Richards t/a Elius Books,
9b Napps Way, Childwall, Liverpool L25 1QE
eliusbooks@blueyonder.co.uk

Design and artwork by UPS Translations, the language
division of United Publicity Services Plc
info@upstranslations.com

Researched and compiled by DV Knox-Richards

Edited by Susan Elkin

ISBN 0952 87125 4

A catalogue record for this book is
available from the British Library.

Printed in the United Kingdom by
Biddles Ltd, Guildford, Surrey

This book is dedicated to John Thaw's daughters:

Melanie-Jane, Abigail and Joanne

„Erbarme Dich mein Gott, um meiner Zähren willen.
Schaue hier Herz und Auge weint vor Dir bitterlich."

The above is taken from Bach's St Matthew's Passion

" I found him to be a complex man, meticulous in detail for whatever
character he was portraying. He often wondered why the ladies
liked him so much, and why he was so successful. A terribly modest man.
I shall miss him."

Contents

Acknowledgements

Elius Books would like to thank the following people for their assistance in providing information and advice in the preparation of this publication. Their meticulous attention to detail and helpful advice has been of enormous benefit and our indebtedness is frankly immensurable.

The British Library, Harvey Bryant, Dominic Cooper (Deputy General Secretary of the Institute of Journalists), writer Colin Dexter, Patrick Dolan, Kevin Dugdale, Barbara Dunne, Marion Donne (The Publishers Association, London), John Knight, National Sound Archive, Dawn Peters, The BBC, Manchester Evening News, Peter Podmore, Joseph Knox, Mr and Mrs C Tudorache, and not forgetting their son, Maxime (age 3), Allan Steele (Aust), and Steven Lodge of Copywriter UK. Finally, Sarah Parkhurst for her patience and understanding with the publisher. It's been a learning curve.

It is, of course impossible to name everyone because one speaks to so many people during the course of any book's production, and perhaps I should refrain from mentioning those whose tempers we have managed to fray a little!

This book is an accolade to those who have assisted us, and to that end all the production team and close friends, are very grateful.

Donald Knox-Richards.
14th November 2002.

On the 21st February 2002, John Thaw died. Not everybody realises that simultaneously, Inspector Morse, Monsignor Renard, Mr Tom, Kavanagh QC., and all the other characters that John Thaw managed to bring to life, in that perfect way of his, perished with him. Within twenty-four hours of his death, I made up my mind to publish this book about him. Despite the trials and tribulations encountered in the preparation of the publication, I have no regrets about doing so. Publishing it has been an absolute pleasure.

I should particularly like to thank Mike Cohen and Andrew Snow, two good friends of mine, without whose support, I do not know where I would have been. They have both, in their own way, been a tremendous boon, and I am most grateful for their help and advice. Now that the book is finished, I earnestly hope that they enjoy the read.

It is a matter of some regret that I could not obtain the input of John Thaw's widow, the actress Sheila Hancock. During the commissioning of *this* book, Ms Hancock has herself come to an agreement with another publisher, to write the biography of her late husband. This is expected to be quite revealing, and my book should not be taken to be intended as competition to her forthcoming book about her famous actor/husband, John Thaw. I sincerely hope that hers will be read widely, like this publication, with thoughts of John Thaw in our minds as we ponder onwards.

I commend this book to all.

Best wishes.

Donald Knox-Richards.
14th November 2002.

Introduction

by Susan Elkin

Susan Elkin is a professional freelance journalist and editor and is Chairman of The Chartered Institute of Journalists Freelance Division. She writes on education, theatre, personalities, music, books, travel – and almost anything which comes her way – for a wide range of newspapers and magazines including *Daily Mail*, *The Independent*, *The Daily Telegraph*, *The Stage*, *Music Teacher* and *Antiques and Collectables*. *Life to the Lees* (Natula 1988) is her biography of craftsman Arthur Romney Green and she has written eleven book-format education reports for Technology Colleges Trust. She also edits two monthly subscription magazines for teachers: *Continuing Professional Development Update* and *Early Years Update*. Susan Elkin lives with her husband in Kent and has two grown-up sons.

John Thaw died in February 2002. He was – and is – mourned by viewers all over the world. Wherever *Inspector Morse*, *Kavanagh QC* or any of the other series, films and one-off dramas he starred in were shown, millions of viewers fell for John Thaw. They admired his understated, quintessentially English, acting style. They adored the apparent Englishness of the settings and plots. Women – and that includes me – were smitten by that not-quite-handsome, but charismatically interesting, lined face, blue eyes and white hair. Thaw's work gave enormous pleasure and drew very large audiences, especially in Britain where, for example, showings of a new episode of *Inspector Morse* routinely attracted 15 million or more viewers.

This book is an appreciation of Thaw's work for, and by his admirers. We asked ten contributors from three continents – journalists, writers, viewers, Thaw fans and, in one case, an eminent doctor – to examine different aspects of Thaw's work and life and to write about it in any way they chose. Some, such as Judith MacLean's study of the United States' response to *A Year in Provence*, Caroline Davies's examination of *Kavanagh QC* from a New Zealand perspective, or Anne Williams's student memories of Thaw on the boards in Liverpool, are very personal.

Others, such as Brian Larsson's account of Thaw's early life, Victoria McKee's interview with Colin Dexter, author of the Morse novels, or Ian Wylie's account of Thaw's late work, are based on face-to-face research and are journalistic in tone. So is Joseph Horodyski's detailed analytical essay on *The Sweeney*. New York-based university teacher, Edna Lief, discusses the appeal of Thaw's work in general, and as Morse in particular, with students and colleagues. Meanwhile, my own contribution on Thaw's appearance on the BBC programme *Desert Island Discs* examines his Morse-like, life-long love affair with classical music.

Chapter 10 is something rather different. We asked a consultant surgeon, Professor J. B. Elder, to write about cancer of the oesophagus, the disease from which the 60-year old Thaw died. It has to be a general essay. Medical ethics prevent Professor Elder from commenting on a specific case. We hope, however, that this background information will give readers – and Thaw admirers – some idea of what John Thaw suffered and the sort of treatment he is likely to have undergone, during the last few months of his life.

Reading and then working on the various contributions as they arrived on my computer screen from all over the world has proved a fascinating and privileged task. I think John Thaw – a great Shakespearean in his RADA, pre-television, days – might, in his characteristically modest way, have enjoyed and been touched by the Cleopatra-esque 'infinite variety' of the affection and respect to which these ten essays are testimony.

The resulting book is a multi-faceted and multifarious appreciation, rather like a Cubist painting. It is a rich mix because each contribution is independently 'shot' from a different angle. Of course, there are overlaps, but such is the range of Thaw's work that there was surprisingly little repetition to edit out. My main job as editor was to arrange the ten contributions and superimpose them one on the other so that, collectively, they present a detailed three-dimensional appreciation of Thaw's achievements.

Because each chapter of *John Thaw 1942–2002: An Appreciation* is written by a different individual, it does not have to be read in any particular order. We begin with Thaw's early life and end with the cause of his death, but each chapter also stands alone. Like a good anthology of poetry, we planned it as a dip-in book as well as something to be read in the sequence in which it is presented.

John Thaw 1942–2002: An Appreciation is not, and makes no claims to be a biography, although inevitably it contains biographical material as the background against which the actor's work is examined. An unauthorised biography was published in 1999. It is said to have deeply upset its subject and his family because of its focus on his childhood after the departure of his mother with suggestions – strongly refuted by Thaw – that his was an unhappy and dysfunctional family background. This contentious book (*John Thaw: the biography* by Stafford Hildred, Andre Deutsch) was republished in paperback in April 2002 shortly after Thaw's death.

Thaw's widow, actress Sheila Hancock, has publicly announced that she is now working on the authorised biography. Ms Hancock's version of her late husband's life will set the record straight and I am looking forward very much to reading it. Obviously, anyone interested in John Thaw's work will want to read both biographies as well as this complementary – and complimentary – Appreciation.

Susan Elkin September 2002

Mimicry and Mistress Quickly

by Brian Larsson

Brian Larsson is a civil engineer and freelance writer. He grew up, as John Thaw did, in the cobbled streets of Manchester at about the same time. Just as John Thaw's family moved to Burnage, so the Larsson family moved to the 'greener pastures' of Bolton. Like Thaw, he just scraped into grammar school so, for several reasons, he feels an affinity with the man he describes as 'arguably the most accomplished actor television has ever produced'. Brian Larsson, who still lives in the Manchester area, has, for many years written for local, regional and national newspapers and magazines, including *The Universe* and *Choice*. For five years he wrote a column for the *Bolton Evening News*.

Pressed into the corner of a crowded, late 1950s Manchester bar, three young friends sat talking quietly but intensely. The two locals were eager for news of the third's new life in London. He spoke in a low voice, as if his news might embarrass him if overheard by other lunchtime drinkers. His story gathered pace and suddenly, oblivious of the crowd, he stepped away from the table and in a theatrical delivery that carried across the bar, gave a speech from *Henry V*, first in the voice of Albert Finney and then of Peter O'Toole, two of his new London contacts, both on their own fast track to fame. The lunchtime crowd hushed. John Thaw completed his speech with a flourish, then sat down and quietly resumed the story of his life in the southern metropolis. The noise across the bar slowly returned. There was a raised eyebrow here, an admiring smile there and the odd snigger. The scene, recalled many years later by one of the old school friends present, was symptomatic of the two distinct and parallel personalities which made up a man who was soon to become, for more than 20 years, one of Britain's best-loved and most admired television actors.

As the war in Europe intensified, industrial Manchester became the target of regular bombing raids. The immediate concern of John Edward Thaw and his wife, Dorothy known as Dolly, was the imminent birth of their first child. In the grid-line terraces of Manchester's West Gorton communities clung together. Each gas-lit, cobbled street had its matriarch. Younger parents would come to her for advice on their sick children, she would lay out the dead before the arrival of the undertaker and often it was she who would bring the newborn into the world.

However, in large, extended families the mother-to-be would often return to her own mother for the birth. John Edward and his wife both came from large families, and so on 3 January, 1942, John Edward Thaw junior was born a short distance away at 9 Norman Grove, Longsight, the home of Dolly's parents, George and Cecilia Ablott.

The young family soon returned to its small terraced house in Stowell Street, tucked away in the shadow of the city centre. West Gorton was typical of most of Manchester's wartime inner city areas. Small rented houses stood in long terraces. Sometimes there was a back alley, sometimes not. Tiny street corner pubs, furtive back street bookies and, in the night, the stuttering clang of shunting goods trains from the Longsight Rail Depot just across Hyde Road.

Young John Thaw was to spend the first five years of his life in West Gorton. His brother, Raymond, was born when John was two years old.

Television was still a luxury and a two-up and two-down terraced house held few attractions to keep children indoors. As there was little or no traffic, play centred around the narrow streets where the children were well within mealtime calling distance. The bigger boys would play soccer against a gable wall or would crouch noisily over the cobbles playing marbles, while the girls skipped or spun tops. For most of their time in West Gorton John and Raymond were too small to join in the serious games, but local communities were close. Sometimes there were street parties for major events, or nearby factories would organise a Christmas outing for the local children. When John Thaw Senior's long distance lorry driving allowed there were the special treats such as a family visit to Belle Vue Zoo, just a short walk away, or to see Father Christmas in the Lewis's Store's grotto in the city centre.

Before the brothers were old enough to join in the big boys' play, the Thaw family left its small terrace and moved to Burnage, a much better residential area well away from the city centre. Burnage was a clear step-up from the terraced, cobbled streets of West Gorton. The neat, brick and tile council houses had picket-fenced gardens back and front. The streets were all called 'drives,' 'avenues' or 'gardens.' Instead of cinder crofts and the railway-shunting yard, there were trees and greenery – even on the council estate. Nearby were plenty of grassy open spaces separating the south-eastern edge of the city from the more affluent north-west Stockport.

The Thaws moved into 4 Daneholm Road. It looked very much like all the other small semi-detached houses on the estate but it was, in fact, a ground floor flat with other people living in the flat above. The living space was probably even less than that in their small Stowell Street terrace, but the area had much more to offer and provided better opportunities to carve out a reasonable life. John and Dorothy soon became friendly with the couple who lived in the upstairs flat, Frank and Gladys Bell. The Bells were to play a significant part in the young brothers' lives.

John began his schooling at Green End Boys' Primary School, a short walk from Daneholm Road across the Burnage Estate. Raymond would not join his elder brother for two years and, during that time, dark clouds began to gather over the Thaws' marriage. Just as Raymond was about to start school, his mother left the family home. The rift was never repaired. She died of cancer some 25 years later. The adult John Thaw would never discuss in detail the circumstances surrounding or the reasons behind his mother's departure. He believed she had simply met someone else, although Dorothy's family disputes that. She returned to live at her parents' house in Norman Grove, Longsight.

Whatever the truth surrounding the break up, at seven years old John and the even younger Raymond were suddenly left with only their father to look after them, a father who had to work to keep the remains of his family together. The sheer determination that the young John Thaw was soon to demonstrate must have been inherited from his father. Despite the emotional turmoil the break up had created, there were practical problems to solve. John senior managed to set up a care regime that in today's world would probably attract the well-meaning disapproval of social workers. In those early post-war years, people were more community-minded. Gladys and Frank Bell helped, so did one of the boys' aunts and, no doubt, several other neighbours were aware of the need. The boys were cared for at a level that at once kept them out of danger, but at the same time developed in them the sense of independence and self-sufficiency that was, in time, to send John to fame and fortune in London and Raymond to a new life on the other side of the world.

Before John had reached his final year at Green End, he had already discovered and begun to develop a talent for entertaining others. Money was a constant problem in the Thaw household, but one of the treats the boys were allowed was the Saturday morning picture show at the nearby Odeon Cinema. John had noticed that one or two youngsters who helped entertain the others until the show started were allowed in free. Even at nine years old, John had the confidence to tell the cinema management, 'I can do that,' and they accepted his offer. Not only had he engineered a scheme where both boys went to the Saturday picture show for the price of one but also, knowingly or not, he had set a path for his future career.

Outside his circle of school friends John was known as a pleasant, but quiet youngster. It was on stage he discovered a new, extrovert personality. He became an entertainer. He found he could keep the children's attention, leading them in noisy, singalong versions of *I've Got a Loverly Bunch of Coconuts*. They would listen and laugh when he repeated jokes he had heard on the radio or when he mimicked well-known voices. Sometimes they would applaud and cheer. And John loved it.

At ten years old he was in his last year at Green End and, during that final year, the boys were to amalgamate with the girls' school to form single Green End Primary School. To celebrate the event a grand musical drama production was planned. At the end of the auditions John was given a leading role. How interesting that, although the play featured mainly children's roles, he was cast as an adult. _Where The Rainbow Ends_ was a fantasy musical featuring lost children, anxious parents, England's St George and a Dragon King. The lead characters included two grown-up 'baddies,' the wicked Aunt Matilda and Uncle Joseph – played by the young John Thaw. The production was a great success and John's stage presence, sharpened by his now regular Saturday morning appearances on stage at The Odeon Cinema, was outstanding.

After leaving primary school John went to the nearby Ladybarn Secondary Modern School to join the 'prep class.' Manchester children spent a year at secondary school before taking the 11-plus examinations that decided whether they stayed at secondary school or progressed to a Grammar or Technical High school. Although John did not shine in his 11-plus, he did just well enough to squeeze into a place at Ducie Technical High School at Moss Side, not very far from his earlier childhood roots near the city centre.

In September 1953, John arrived for his first term at Ducie High School. News of his stage prowess as an Odeon Cinema entertainer and as Uncle Joseph in _Where the Rainbow Ends_ may well have preceded him. He very soon found himself preparing for a part in the annual school play. In that first year, it was to be Shakespeare's _Henry V_. First-year boys were sometimes involved in the school play, but it was unusual for one of them to be offered a part and even more unusual for a boy so young to be given a small, but significant, role. John played Mistress Quickly.

Throughout his youth, he would take advantage, whenever he could, of the fact that he looked much older than he actually was. However, as Mistress Quickly he was not only an adult, but also the colourful, larger-than-life hostess of the Boar's Head Tavern, the setting for several rumbustious low-life scenes. He carried it off, even the Shakespearean dialogue, with the sort of aplomb that he had already demonstrated in other places.

From his first performance at Ducie High School he established himself as a confident and competent performer. He appeared in every subsequent school play, taking leading parts long before he reached the fifth form despite the fact that the 'star' roles had always previously been the province of the boys in their final year.

Beyond school, John was constantly on the lookout for other opportunities to practice his entertainment skills. He knew by then that performing in public was something he could do. He knew he was good at it and loved the praise he earned from others. Local summer events, especially those designed to attract families, such as Burnage Rose Queen Day, often included a talent competition. Wherever there was a talent competition, there was John Thaw with his comic singing, impersonations and jokes. Whether the judges loved him for the polish of his performance or the surprising, and no doubt endearing, on-cue transformation from a quiet and shy young man to a confident, extrovert entertainer is not clear. What is clear is that John had begun to run away with most of the prizes in the area.

A local dancing and music school had several talented young pupils, one of whom was an excellent pianist, as well as being the only male dancer in the school. He, too, enjoyed the talent contests and had a record of success of which he was very proud. However, despite his tutored talent, the new kid on the block – the self-taught entertainer – began to relegate him to the status of runner-up. The young pianist's cousin recalled, many years later, that the other boy was 'very, very, miffed'.

Raymond Thaw, at the age of ten, was meanwhile developing a talent for sport and had no time for books. His older brother had no interest whatsoever in sport. John's passions were literature, drama, and reading. The two were to be described later by a good friend as 'like chalk and cheese'. When John's close friends at Ducie High played football on the cinder crofts around the school, John was there too. He would be on the sidelines reading a book.

He did not lack academic ability. He had passed his 11-plus against expectations. However, his notable achievements at Ducie High were to be restricted by his single-minded interest in some subjects to the exclusion of others. As well as rejecting sport, he disliked the sciences and jettisoned them in favour of English literature and history at the very first opportunity. John had started well, but good marks in his 'interesting' subjects were offset by poor displays in those for which he had no time. As a result, he slipped down the streaming levels as he progressed through the school until he was able to concentrate his attention on the arts. Even then, a close friend recalled, 'John and I, and the rest of the gang, did what we had to do, and got away with as much as we possibly could'.

Despite his intense interest in literature and drama, he was still very much 'one of the lads' among his peers. The same close friend, Peter Podmore, remembers John as a 'nice, easy-going person. No different from anyone else. An ordinary bloke with no edge about him.' Another member of the Thaw 'gang' recalls the times just before examinations when even John and the others realised that they needed to study. They would take their books and their free milk down into the warmth and quiet of the boiler room. Even so, most of the 'boiler room time' seems to have been spent listening to and laughing at John revelling in his captive audience by giving uncannily accurate impersonations of their teachers.

Friends remember girl-baiting as a popular pastime and John would join in. Ducie High was in fact two schools on the same site, boys on the ground floor and girls on the first. There were constant attempts to circumvent the rules which banned contact between the two. Another close school friend, Harvey Bryant, insists that on a one-to-one basis, John was exceptionally shy with girls. Nevertheless, it became obvious that he particularly admired a girl called Alison Lui whose parents had a well-known Chinese Laundry business in the Strangeways area of Manchester. Another contemporary, John Knight, was well aware that Alison was the only girl that John ever showed a real interest in during their time at Ducie High. Both agree that he was far too shy with girls to do anything about it. Neither friend remembers him ever taking her out. Even when they brought along girlfriends to a night on the town, John would be there alone.

His painful reticence with the opposite sex was in stark contrast to the self-confidence he had in the things he considered he could do well. Harvey Bryant invited him to a birthday party for his cousin. John had seen this girl before and made some admiring remark. Adults had been diverted elsewhere and the house was packed with 14- and 15-year-olds. John's self-assurance saw him turn up in drainpipe trousers, a V-neck sweater and a cravat. He was smoking a cigarette from a long cigarette holder. Harvey's plan was to get John and his cousin together. He had even primed his cousin in advance. She liked the look of John Thaw despite his clothes. The plan failed. John was too shy to get beyond a mumbled 'hello' and a glance at the floor.

His awkward reserve with girls never affected his uncanny ability to snap into his 'entertainer' personality at the drop of a hat. On one occasion before an evening out with Harvey and some friends, he went to Harvey's home straight from school. The house was full of relatives celebrating his grandmother's birthday. John knew none of them. The two boys felt obliged to stay for a short time and sat around the room hoping they would not attract too much attention before they could decently disappear. The uncles and aunts began to show an interest in Harvey's friend. The boys decided that the only way they were going to get out quickly was for John to 'perform,' after which they could both take the opportunity to 'exit stage left'. John had not, of course, prepared anything – but that was no barrier. He stood up in the middle of the room, the crowd parted like the Red Sea and he launched into a long Shakespearean speech full of expressive gestures and wide-ranging modulation. What was even more startling, Harvey remembers, was that the speech was delivered in the very distinctive voice of a well-known classical actor of the time, Brandsby Williams. The impersonation must have been close to perfect. Williams was almost 90 years old, but the voice was instantly recognised by everyone in the room. At the end of the speech, there was a short silence followed by tumultuous applause.

The school paths of the two Thaw brothers had now parted. Raymond remained at Ladybarn Secondary School, having failed his 11-plus. As John made his way through Ducie High and collected a completely new circle of friends, he was nevertheless very careful to make sure he always did the right thing by Raymond. When John was 14 years old, two local youth organisations were trying very hard to persuade him to join. One was Burnage Youth Club, for which he had a preference. Among other things, the club ran a concert party, well known in the area for its 'gang show' type concerts, which toured around South Manchester charity venues. John said he would join, but only on one condition: Raymond, two years younger, must be allowed to join too. The leaders of Burnage Youth Club were well aware of John Thaw the performer so, despite strict regulations requiring a minimum age of 14, they turned a blind eye to Raymond's age and John had found another regular outlet for his entertainer's talents.

He immediately became an important part of the youth club. He easily adapted his role as Saturday morning picture show compere to become Burnage Concert Party Master of Ceremonies, despite being younger than most of the other members. Barbara Dunne was a member at the time. She remembers John as a 'pleasant, much laid-back, very nice but shy young man. He never chatted. Sometimes the conversation was hard going because he would not volunteer a contribution.' She said he never talked about feelings or ambitions and whatever was in his head would never come out of its own accord.

John's main role as Master of Ceremonies involved introductions and filling in between the frantic scene-shifting behind the curtain. Barbara recalls that John preferred the compere's role to that of acting in the show itself. He had, of course, a ready-made store of jokes, songs and mimicry from his Odeon Cinema days. He was very reliable. He often had to re-arrange his home life because of his father's job, but he missed few rehearsals. Once, he turned up to one performance with his leg in plaster from toe to thigh. Barbara

Dunne remembers the occasion clearly. He could hardly walk, but he insisted on compering the show sitting on a stool at the side of the stage with his broken leg projected out in front of him. Being the secretive and somewhat introverted John Thaw, he told nobody how he had done it.

The concert party shows were a yearly event performed for a week in the hall at Green End School. After the main performance, no opportunity was missed to take the show around the district to charity events in hospitals and town halls. It even went to Strangeways Prison in Manchester. The concert party, his deep involvement in drama at school, the talent contests and what Barbara Dunne recalls as 'busking around the town' meant a lot of performing. Fate was drawing John gently but firmly towards a life he was later to acknowledge, 'was not the sort of thing lorry drivers' sons were into'.

His independent self-assurance did occasionally waver. Sometimes he wanted old friends with him. He tried very hard to persuade his friend John Knight to join the concert party, dragging him along to a rehearsal and getting him involved in the finale. John Knight was careful not to go again. Years later, when John Thaw, fresh from RADA, was struggling to find work he asked his other good friend, Harvey Bryant, if he would join him in London.

During the final year at Ducie High School, fewer subjects studied meant several free periods during the week. John and his friends always used the time imaginatively, often ignoring the fact that they were forbidden to leave the school grounds. A memorable 'gang' trip to see Elvis Presley in a matinee performance of *Jailhouse Rock* at the Theatre Royal, a short bus ride away, was one of the highlights. Had they been caught the recriminations would have been very serious.

More significant, perhaps, were John's surreptitious daytime visits to a city centre pub to see his mother. He took Harvey Bryant with him at least twice, although he told Sue Lawley on *Desert Island Discs* in 1990 that he never saw his mother again after she had left home, apart from a single occasion when he was about 40. Coming out of an examination and with the rest of the afternoon supposedly destined for study, John suddenly suggested, 'Let's go and see my mother. She works at The Shakespeare.' The pub was in the city centre next to the Lewis's Store where John and Raymond's mother had taken them as little children to visit Father Christmas. When Thaw and Bryant arrived, it was after closing time. John knocked on the door and his mother invited the boys in. She was clearing tables in preparation for opening later in the evening and was obviously pleased to see John. Harvey remembers her giving them sandwiches left over from lunchtime. They went again at John's suggestion several days later. John knew the exact location of the pub so it seems unlikely that his two visits with Harvey Bryant were the only ones he made.

Throughout his time at Green End and Ducie High School and among his schoolmates, teachers and friends at Burnage Youth Club, he seldom, if ever, spoke about his mother. Among his closer school friends, he would mention his father, but only if the subject was raised. Nevertheless, they knew he idolised his father. John's reticence about his mother and his tremendous admiration for his father's efforts in bringing up his two sons made Harvey Bryant suspect that those visits to The Shakespeare indicated that John sometimes felt deeply unhappy at missing a part of his childhood.

John liked the same sort of music as his friends – skiffle and rock 'n' roll. Later he would develop a taste for classical music, not unlike the character who was to become his most enduring television role. But at 16 years old and looking much older, the only resemblance to Inspector Morse was a slight limp and a moderate liking for beer. He could never have been described as a heavy drinker, but he developed a liking for jazz which could be heard live in the many pubs surrounding Manchester's Smithfield Market. The area became a frequent haunt of John Thaw and John Knight.

John Knight was envied as the owner of a two-spool Grundig tape recorder. It was the size of a small suitcase. In 1958, it was considered to be state-of-the-art. The two friends would spend an evening recording rock 'n' roll, skiffle and jazz from Radio Luxembourg hosted by the young Jimmy Saville. The station's crackly reception would ebb and flow and in poor weather would disappear altogether. On those occasions, they would tape-record from records, jazz if they were John Knight's, Shakespearean speeches by Laurence Olivier if they were John Thaw's. John Knight's father sometimes looked at his son's choice of pal through narrowed eyes and scratched his head.

Their preference, however, was live music in the 'grown-up' atmosphere of a smoky pub. If John Thaw had no commitment at Burnage Youth Club and his father was at home for Raymond, the two friends would be off to Smithfield. Musicians with bookings later that evening at other venues, such as The Bodega, would often meet up in Shudehill's Turks Head or Swan Street's George and Dragon with its tiny stage perched halfway up the wall. A jam session would invariably break out. Tapping their feet in a corner of the bar, complete with pint of beer and obligatory cigarette, would be two young men.

From his first venture on to the stage at The Odeon Cinema, John Thaw knew what he wanted to do with his life. He wanted to be an actor. His brother Raymond could not remember him ever wanting to do anything else. John told Harvey Bryant, 'One day I'll be on *This is Your Life*'. If he had a plan of action to achieve his aim, then, typically, he did not reveal it to any of his friends.

His father was now working as an ambulance driver and one of his duties was to chauffeur Councillor Mrs Kingsmill Jones to and from the Duchess of York Hospital where she was a board member. She was also a governor of Ducie High School and knew from her friend Sam Hughes, the headmaster, that her chauffeur's son was a 'star' performer at Ducie. Left to his own devices and relying on his own determination, John Thaw might well have carved out for himself a successful niche in theatre and television. However, his talent had attracted influential friends and they were instrumental in persuading the Royal Academy of Dramatic Art (RADA) to offer him an audition. When RADA recognised his potential and offered him a place, Sam Hughes and Mrs Kingsmill Jones would make sure that the door to his future career was not slammed shut by lack of funds. Manchester's Education Committee agreed to provide a grant to cover the fees.

In the final year at Ducie High, the history and drama teacher, John Lee, had two protégés, John Thaw and his friend Kevin Dugdale. The school production that year was to be *Macbeth*, with John Thaw in the lead and Kevin as Macduff. Kevin recalls John Lee telling him confidentially that he had a friend at RADA who had agreed to come to Manchester especially to watch the performance. He said that it was important that Kevin performed well. There can be little doubt that John Lee had the same confidential conversation with John Thaw. With the help of Lee's near professional standards of production and the brilliance of his two 'stars,' the play must have made an impact. A short time later, with the support of headmaster Sam Hughes, Lee told John Thaw that he had secured for him an audition at RADA if he wanted it. Of course he did. By then, John Lee's other protégé had decided on another career.

John's stage appearances had soon taught him that his accustomed conversational speech was not suitable on stage. He needed different qualities of diction and articulation. His talent for mimicry helped. He was aware that, on stage, his Mancunian accent was merely subdued, not eliminated. His familiarity with some of the great dramatic speeches he had on record, especially those of his idol Olivier, must have convinced him that he would stand a better chance at RADA if he could do something about his accent. He told Barbara Dunne that he was desperate for some sort of elocution guidance, but as always, he could not afford proper lessons. Barbara had had a certain amount of speech training and was already teaching at a local school. She offered to help John who gratefully accepted. Joyce Palin, who ran the school, had had professional acting experience. When Barbara told her of John's coming audition, Joyce offered him drama lessons. She also promised to coach him in what RADA would be looking for. Again, John gratefully accepted. This reticent young man, who found it difficult to talk about himself and who was often uncomfortable with girls, clearly had an unconscious charm which made people want to help him.

As the audition date approached, anticipation and the excitement were tempered with practical difficulties. How was he to get to London? If he were offered a place, how was he to pay the fees? He had the support of his father who insisted on going with him to London. 'We drove down in a van. My uncle's van. My brother and I were stuck in the back of this van for what seemed like days going down to London. We could not afford the train fare. When we arrived at RADA I jumped out of the back of the van, went and did the audition, then got back in the van and set off for what seemed like another two days.'

It was worth it. Behind the doors of RADA, John had read Othello, received the offer of a place and been sworn to secrecy about being under age. His London audition persuaded RADA's principal, John Fernald, to offer him a place even though, at 16, he was more than two years below the usual age for admission.

After leaving Ducie High School, John needed to fill the summer of 1958 before his first term at RADA, which would not begin until September. Aware of the state of the family finances and with typical single mindedness, John decided to work through the summer. Manchester's Smithfield Market was then only a short distance from his old home in West Gorton, but it was a world away from life as a Moss Side schoolboy and even further away from life as it was to be at drama school. The market, in Manchester's Northern Quarter, was a vast, cast-iron arched building adjacent to the city centre. At three or four o'clock in the morning, the first of the day's wagons would roll up loaded with fresh produce. Gangs of casual porters would appear, as if from nowhere, ready to off-load the wagons.

John's job at Smithfield was to stack the newly-arrived fruit on Thelwell's Wholesale Fruit Stall. He was also expected to 'pitch' the goods to the local shopkeepers who were looking for the day's best buys. Market porters' pay was casual and insecure. What John earned was regular but almost negligible. The rewards of the job amounted to no more than the occasional 'slinger' – a blemished apple or cauliflower tossed to one side. Neither was work as a humble fruit stacker without its dangers.

Pat Dolan worked at the market in and around the Thelwell stall for many years and got to know the 'quiet young feller' finding his way in his first job. He remembers John Thaw as 'a helpful kid who would willingly do what he was asked by the older porters. He would not start a conversation, unless you brought him into it. He always seemed to have a bit more going on up here,' said Pat, pointing a finger at his head.

John's earlier broken leg had left him with a limp that was to stay with him for the rest of his life. Lifting and stacking loaded apple crates was difficult enough without a 'suspect' leg. His inexperience soon caught up with him. He slipped and badly gashed his chin on one of the binding wires. First aid facilities were rudimentary. Pat Dolan, improvising as best he could, helped stem the blood flow until John was taken off to hospital to have the wound stitched. The scar remained.

'There was this big black mole too,' said Pat. 'It was the size of a thumbnail over his left eyebrow. I think he was a bit embarrassed by it. When you spoke to him, he would put his hand over it or turn his head away slightly.' John was later to have the mole removed, leaving only the bruise-coloured mark over his left eye. Characteristically, he never told any of his old Manchester friends when or why it had gone. The slight residual limp, the scar on his chin and a blue-black blemish over his left eye were, in time, to become familiar to millions of television viewers across the world.

The early start at Smithfield often meant an early afternoon finish. Many of the porters and stall helpers would go to one of the local pubs for a drink, but Pat Dolan remembers that John 'didn't go with the market guys. He looked older than 16 and I knew he went in pubs from the general talk and banter that went on during the day. But he must have gone for a drink on his own or maybe with his other mates.' Pat, who lived close to the market, tried to give John the benefit of his experience of the local pubs. 'Don't go in the 'top' Kings, but the White Bear on Swan Street is all right, and The Vincent just across Oldham Road.' In fact, John already knew most of the local pubs through his interest in skiffle, rock 'n' roll, and live jazz.

Several years ago, the then head of Ducie High School was invited to an awards ceremony where she found herself talking to John Thaw for half an hour or so about his childhood. She said he was 'very pleasant, very polite, very friendly'. She sometimes felt, however, that she had to drive the conversation. She thought John 'found it difficult to offer anecdotes about his time at Ducie High'. She left a telephone number in case he ever wanted to contact the school, but she didn't think he ever would.

On one occasion, he met some of his old concert party friends in a local pub before he appeared at The Rex in Wilmslow. One of them asked him how he was coping with fame. John said, 'With great difficulty. I love the work, but I hate all the publicity. I like to go home, shut the door and take the phone off the hook. That's my world. I don't want to know.' He told her he avoided hotels if he could. 'If I have two days off, I'll go home.'

One of his old school friends bumped into John in the centre of Manchester. He was coming out of a pub that they both knew from their days as 16-year-old jazz enthusiasts. 'John was wearing thigh high leather boots, a silk scarf, a black cape and was smoking from a long cigarette holder.'

In his off-stage persona, the young John Thaw was helpful, polite, quiet, somewhat reserved, uncomfortable with girls and had difficulty talking about himself. Then the curtain would rise to a fanfare and the audience would see a funny comedian, a brilliant mimic, an engaging compere or a budding young actor carrying off with confidence the roles of old Uncle Joseph or the bawdy hostess of the Boar's Head Tavern. John Thaw carried into his adult life most of the characteristics that marked out the young man finding his way through a Manchester childhood. Along the path, with a little help from his friends, a little luck, the confidence and guts to give it a try and an enormous talent, he became, through Regan, Morse, Kavanagh, Mister Tom and many others, a television legend.

A tribute from Merseyside

by Anne Williams

Anne Williams, a mail order company courier, has always lived in Liverpool, the city of her birth. There, she brought up three daughters, who are now grown up. Having attended one of Liverpool's best grammar schools, she has always been an avid reader, theatre lover and is passionate about good acting. Anne Williams remembers, in her youth, seeing Lawrence Olivier, John Gielgud, Sybil Thorndyke, Lewis Casson, Vivienne Leigh and Peter Wyngarde at The Shakespeare and The Royal Court theatres in Liverpool, as well as admiring the work of the young John Thaw at the Liverpool Playhouse. Television – and the good drama such as the series and films starring John Thaw – became a substitute for theatre when three young children largely confined her to the house.

I first saw John Thaw at the Liverpool Playhouse. I was in the sixth form and he was a young actor, one year older than I.

When I was a teenager – but we were not called teenagers then – most young people were into jazz, or skiffle or rock 'n' roll. Then there was a new group called the Beatles, who redefined what became known as pop. I enjoyed music, but my real love was theatre. My heroes were actors and my idea of a good night out was a visit to the Liverpool Playhouse or the Royal Court. I was, apparently, born with a love of acting. My mother used to say that I sat through Olivier's film of *Henry V* at the age of two. I cannot remember that, but I do remember going to the cinema at least once a week, but liking only the film stars that I regarded as good actors.

We went to pantomimes every Christmas and then, in Festival of Britain year, 1951, when I was eight, I was taken to see the Royal Ballet at the Royal Court Theatre in Liverpool. I was enthralled and can clearly recall seeing Moira Shearer in an excerpt from *The Sleeping Beauty* and a rising young star called Margot Fonteyn in an excerpt from *La Cenerentola*, by Rossini (she had an injury and could only dance demi-pointe). This was the beginning of a lifelong love of theatre. I can also remember begging to be allowed to stay up late to see the end of *1984* starring Peter Cushing and Yvonne Mitchell on what was a very primitive black and white television set, but at the time it seemed like a minor miracle. Dad took my side in spite of the warning that the play was unsuitable for children (I think I was about ten) and I was allowed to watch. I think I can say I had an instinct for a good performance and an innate love of drama.

At 11 I won a scholarship to one of the best girls' grammar schools in Liverpool and discovered that among the extra-curricular activities was a dramatic society run by a nun called Sister Therese. I think she could have had a career as a director in secular life. She was simply terrific and enthused us all with her love of theatre. In fact, three of the girls in the society at the same time as I, are now professionals (Judy Bennett, Maureen O'Brien and Eileen O'Brien). I took part in school productions, including excerpts from Shakespeare and *Pride and Prejudice*, increasing my respect for the professional actors.

When I was 16, the Liverpool Playhouse started a scheme called The Playgoers Club, which offered a discount if a group of people booked tickets for every production. Our school entered the scheme and I became the secretary of the club. This simply meant that I collected the names of people who wanted to go to any production, ordered the tickets, which were sent to school, and then collected the money and distributed them. So for two years, I saw virtually every production at the Playhouse – and John Thaw.

The Liverpool Playhouse had been known for many years as a breeding ground for future stars. Michael Redgrave met his wife Rachel Kempson at the Playhouse and, in the early 1960s, it was one of the best repertory theatres in the country. During those two years, I remember seeing Richard Briers, Pauline Yates, Robert James, Terence Knapp and Caroline Blakiston, as well as John.

However, it was John who stood out for me. He had an edge, a brooding presence, almost a James Dean attitude, and a hint of danger. In those days, he was definitely more Regan than Morse. He also had that little extra something which nobody can really define except as star quality. Put him stage left in the corner and your eye would be drawn to him. I discovered that he had won the season at the Playhouse as one of the top students of his year at the Royal Academy of Dramatic Art (RADA), which did not surprise me. I fell hopelessly for John and bored all my school friends rigid enthusing about him. He was not conventionally handsome, but he had a face you could not forget and a charisma which crossed the footlights. At school, we were divided into John Thaw fans and Richard Briers fans. It is, I think, a tribute to our good judgement that both men went on to such successful careers.

After enjoying the play, we quite often dashed round to the stage door to see the actors leaving and it is my constant regret that I never plucked up the courage to speak to John. Some of the actors came out positively looking for autographs to sign and fans to speak to – but not John. He tended to scuttle away with his head down in the hopes of not being recognised. I now know how shy he was and how difficult he always found it to deal with adulation and attention, even when he became a big star, so in a way I am glad I never embarrassed him.

When he left Liverpool, I, of course, had no idea why. I assumed that his season had finished, but now I know that he was not entirely happy with the set-up. If the Everyman had existed then, he would probably have been happier there. The early 1960s was a time of change in the theatre when acting was becoming much less of a middle class preserve. John was definitely part of the new wave. The Playhouse did some very good stuff, but perhaps it was a little conventional for an 18-year-old, self-professed working class actor. (It is, of course, possible that John was youthfully intolerant of some of the older actors.) The Playhouse was not the same for me after John had left. I still enjoyed the plays, but there was a spark missing.

It was not long before I saw John again. He was in a small, but telling, part in the 1962 film *The Loneliness of the Long Distance Runner* starring his great friend from RADA, Tom Courtenay. John looked very James Dean with a wonderful teddy boy haircut. Ironically, the working class speech he had struggled so hard to eradicate was reinstated for the part of a tough Borstal boy. This was, I suppose, the beginning of the hard man image, which seemed to dominate his early career, although he also had a decided, if sometimes overlooked talent for comedy.

A couple of years later I read in the *TV Times* of the advent of a television series called *Redcap*. The name of the star, although not well known to most viewers then, filled me with hope. Surely this must be 'my' John Thaw? Indeed, it was. He looked much as I remembered him, but with a very military haircut. *Redcap* was unusual in at least two ways. It was a cop series but, in this case, the cop was a military policeman. In the early 1960s, we were not far past the end of compulsory National Service. Even World War II seemed quite recent and few conscripts had fond memories of the redcaps. So it was a brave decision to screen the series about Sergeant Mann. It was also unusual in that it had only one star. Most crime series have either a main star and his subordinate or friend, such as Poirot and Captain Hastings, or two equal partners like Cagney and Lacey. *Redcap* had only one main character, which meant that the series would stand or fall on John's performance and his ability to win over the audience.

He was also the youngest leading man in a major television series at the time. He rose to the challenge magnificently. Viewers and critics enjoyed the programme, which ran to two 13-week series and established John as a new star.

He seemed to have found in television the perfect medium for his talent. As a young mother whose husband often worked away, I found getting to the theatre difficult. Television was a godsend for me, as it was for many people in the same circumstances. This was the time at which television sets became affordable and desirable for the majority of people and its main rival was cinema. It was also before the arrival of so-called dumbing-down and reality TV. What I remember most about the 1960s and 1970s was the abundance of good drama screened and the number of excellent actors and actresses working in it.

Like all the best actors, Thaw made it look easy. You never caught John obviously acting because he was so natural. Television is a very unforgiving medium. Because it relies a lot on close-ups and a very subtle style of acting, at its best it makes viewers feel that they are simply eavesdropping on events and not watching a performance at all. This was what John did so well. His characters always seemed real. Appearing in so many series enabled him to develop the characters over a period of time. He did not so much play a part as create a character that we felt we knew. I believe he was the best television actor of his generation and that only John could have appeared in so many television series and made each character different and distinct. I think he qualifies for the title of the best television actor ever because he worked in the heyday of television drama.

John also appeared regularly in one-off television productions and was always a joy to watch, but it was in 1974 that he really began to make an impact on the general public and to achieve star status. An Armchair Cinema production introduced us to *Regan*. John had found the character that was to jump-start his television career. His first words as Regan, 'Get yer trousers on, you're nicked,' are still instantly recognised today, and phrases like 'We're the Sweeney, son, and we haven't had our dinner yet,' have passed into folklore. True, the writing came first, but you need a John Thaw to deliver lines like that and make them both funny and menacing at the same time. With John, the character was never all on the surface. You always felt what was going on behind the eyes.

Regan was an instant hit and led to the drama series *The Sweeney* and two feature films: *Sweeney!* in 1975 and *Sweeney II* in 1978. Regan was a hard man doing a hard job, but somehow we all knew that he was, at heart, one of the good guys. And John could convey those hidden depths with a look or a sigh. Subtlety might not have been Jack Regan's forte but it was John Thaw's. He gave Regan a universal appeal: men wanted to be him and women wanted to marry him.

The comedy series *Home to Roost* in 1985 showed viewers a different side of John Thaw. He played a divorced father struggling to cope when his teenage son, played by Reece Dinsdale, decides that, after many years apart, he wants to live with his father for the foreseeable future. John had appeared in many comedies on stage, but television audiences were somewhat surprised to find he could play comedy just as well as the more serious stuff they were used to. The series, written by Eric Chappell, was recorded in front of a studio audience, a new experience for John, but one with which he coped with habitual professionalism. It was also notable as one of the few occasions when his real-life wife, Sheila Hancock, appeared with him as guest star in one of the episodes. It was a hit with both viewers and critics alike and ended with John's character, Henry Willow, thankfully seeing his son off to university.

In 1987, John played what I think was his greatest film role, a cameo in *Cry Freedom*, the story of South African freedom fighter Steve Biko, who was beaten to death in police custody. John played Kruger, the South African Chief of Police, in an important scene with Kevin Kline as Donald Woods, the newspaper editor who exposed the story. John's accent was faultless and he exuded evil while appearing to be an urbane, sophisticated and civilised man. It was an awe-inspiring performance.

It was also in 1987 that John became the character for which he will always be best remembered. As Chief Inspector Morse, he was a joy to watch. Slightly heavier than the young man I had seen at the Liverpool Playhouse, now with the trademark white hair but still sporting blue eyes to die for, he enslaved a million middle-aged women and many younger ones, too. His success in the role was to be worldwide. In the United States, especially, the show was very popular and provided more thoughtful viewing than most violent American cop shows.

Morse proved what I had always felt about John. He did not play a part, he created a character. I had read none of the Inspector Morse books when I watched the first episode, but I bought the first two the next day. I was surprised to find that author Colin Dexter's original Sergeant Lewis was a middle-aged Welshman with a passion for Oxford United football team and egg and chips and that Morse had dark hair and drove a Lancia. Already, it had become impossible to imagine Morse being any different from John Thaw's brilliant portrayal.

I thought that the dramatisations had complicated plots, but when I started reading the books, I realised just how much they had been simplified. The original stories were extensively adapted and many later episodes were not based on Colin Dexter's books at all. However, the series remained true to the spirit of the originals and was unmissable for millions of viewers. Like *Redcap*, *Inspector Morse* was a bit of a gamble at the beginning. Television executives were doubtful that any drama could hold an audience for two hours, but the production team felt, quite rightly, that the stories could not be compressed into anything less. They felt that a programme of sufficient quality would hold the audience and they were proved right. My husband used to call *Inspector Morse* the two-hour silence because, he said, nobody was allowed to speak while it was on.

The complicated plots absorbed viewers, the Oxford settings looked wonderful, but it was John's performance as the grumpy, but loveable Morse that really made the series something very special. Colin Dexter himself was so delighted with John's performance that, in his subsequent books, Morse acquired white hair and a Jaguar. He became so like John Thaw that it is now impossible to separate the written Morse from the television version.

Inspector Morse ran to six series. Its popularity continued to grow and it seemed as if it could go on forever. John began to worry about being too old to play a serving policeman and it was becoming increasingly difficult for Kevin Whately to fit the part of Lewis into his work schedule. Like Dennis Waterman a decade earlier, working with John had made him a star.

I don't think I ever saw an episode of *Inspector Morse* that fell below the excellent standards set by the early episodes. It was a rarity among television series in that each one seems to get better. It never became repetitive or formulaic. I find it very difficult to pick out a favourite episode simply because the quality was so consistently high, but the two episodes set outside Oxford were quite special.

'Promised Land' took Morse and Lewis to Australia on the track of a super grass who had been relocated there with a new identity. Morse was very uncomfortable in the outback and notable as the only person wearing a suit and tie the whole time. His only happy moment there was a visit to the Sydney Opera House. Lewis, on the other hand, took to the life like a duck to water and even muttered speculatively about emigration. The climax of the episode was nail-biting with Morse walking out alone to meet a gunman holding a young girl hostage. A mistake by a local policeman leads to a shoot-out in which the bad guy is killed – the very thing Morse was trying to prevent. John's expression as his shirt and face are sprayed with blood expressed sorrow, anger and frustration all at once without his having to say a word. It was a masterpiece of acting.

In contrast, the other 'foreign' episode, 'Death of the Self', sent Morse and Lewis to Italy, where Morse loved the weather, the food, the atmosphere and the opera. Poor Lewis hated everything, could not understand what people were saying and just wanted to go home. It was probably the most beautiful-looking episode, set in Verona and with a breathtaking finale in the open-air opera house. It was also quite a treat for John who shared Morse's love of opera.

What was originally intended to be the final episode of *Inspector Morse*, 'Twilight of the Gods,' also featured an opera singer, but this time the setting was back in Oxford and boasted a guest appearance by no less a person than Sir John Gielgud, himself a professed Morse fan.

My favourite episode in terms of the acting has to be 'Masonic Mysteries' in which Morse is framed for the murder of his latest girlfriend. We all know how the brilliant Morse had a tendency to latch on to a suspect purely because of a hunch and how difficult it was to persuade him that the evidence did not back him up. In this episode, this tendency is turned against him by a very clever opponent who persuades him that the Masons are out to get him. It is Lewis's expertise with computers – Morse could barely manage to turn one on – that provides the breakthrough, mainly because the real killer is using computer hacking to alter records. Apart from the clever plot in which the real killer is for a long time thought to be dead, this episode is notable for the quality of the acting. Now famous as Senator Palpatine in the *Star Wars* prequels, the inestimable Ian McDiarmid played the villain, Hugo de Vries. Ian is one of the very few actors who could share a screen with John without being overwhelmed. Their ten-minute duel of words is a joy.

Although the sixth series was the last, Morse was too good to lose altogether and he returned in 1995 in a two-hour special adapted from the newly published book *The Way Through the Woods*. Both John Thaw and Kevin Whately were apprehensive as to whether *Inspector Morse* would be as successful after an absence of three years, but they were soon reassured. Viewers were delighted to see Morse and Lewis back and a one-off Morse adventure then became a yearly event with 'The Daughters of Cain', 'Death is Now My Neighbour' and my favourite 'The Wench is Dead' following. The latter even survived the absence of Lewis when Kevin Whately was not available to play the part. A young constable, PC Adrian Kershaw, is drafted in to do the legwork for Morse who is confined to a hospital bed but manages to prove that innocent men were hanged for murder some hundred years earlier. The episode ended somewhat ambiguously with Morse discussing retirement with his boss. It left us wondering if we would ever see him again.

I read all the later Morse books as they were published and enjoyed the speculation about his first name as much as anyone, although I was a little surprised when Colin Dexter actually revealed it. He had always said that he would do so only in the last book. Dexter had said, apparently, that he realised that he could drop dead at any time and the 'last book' would then never be written.

I do not know if this was the thinking behind the plot of *The Remorseful Day*, but when it was published I was horrified to hear that Morse had been killed off. I will never understand why he could not simply be left to enjoy an honourable retirement and I still have not read the book. I could not bring myself to watch the episode when it was televised and now I doubt that I ever will. If I found it hard to contemplate Morse's demise before, it would definitely be too painful to watch now that John is no longer with us.

With every new police series appearing on television being hailed as the new Morse, it is apparent just how fine *Inspector Morse* became. Repeats serve only to emphasise how far ahead of all its rivals it was and still is. I don't believe that there will ever be a new Morse. Everything about the programme set new and, as yet unmatched, standards: Barrington Pheloung's theme tune based on the Morse code for Morse, the writing, production values and, above all, the acting. It was truly innovative television by which the standard of all detective series is now judged. A great deal of the credit for that has to go to John Thaw for his outstanding work.

Although it is impossible to contemplate anybody else's playing Morse, there was more to John Thaw, the actor, than this one part. Many soap stars and actors in long-running series have found, to their cost, that being closely identified with a popular character has meant that the public was unable to accept them in another role. You might think that John Thaw was so closely identified with Morse that he would have had just that problem. Somehow, John made every character his own and each was different from the last.

Kavanagh QC was a perfect example. He first played the part of the successful barrister after the sixth series of Morse, but before the specials started. Sporting a longer, classier hairstyle to accommodate the hated wig and with a moderated Manchester accent, Kavanagh managed to be a very different personality from Morse. He was a working class man made good in a profession which was once the province of the middle classes, and this made him, perhaps, the character with the closest to parallels to John's own life. John Thaw was always acutely aware of his working class background. His down-to-earth attitude to his work was something the public sensed and responded to. Everybody felt they could share a pint with Jack Regan, although Morse's intellect did put him on a slightly different level. Even John confessed that he would have been overawed by Morse's brain if he had met him in real life.

Of course, nobody gets it right all the time and John, as he admitted himself, had a disaster in 1993 with *A Year* in *Provence*. Based on the best-seller by Peter Mayle, it appeared to have all the ingredients for success, but the 12-week series was a decided flop. Nobody really could understand why. It certainly had nothing to do with the acting, but it did suffer a scheduling problem. It was put up against *The Darling Buds of May*, already an extremely popular and well-established series starring David Jason, an actor who was also a favourite with the viewing public. *The Darling Buds of May* was also a rural escapist drama, but set in the English countryside. Both series probably appealed to the same audience who were, therefore, forced to choose and *A Year in Provence* lost out to the established favourite.

I would watch John Thaw reading somebody's laundry list, but even I did find *A Year in Provence* a bit of a one-joke story and after a few episodes, the joke began to wear thin. As John said it was a disaster but everybody is allowed one. The year was redeemed for him by the award of the CBE from the Queen who let it be known she had watched *Inspector Morse* as well as *A Year in Provence*.

I missed seeing *Goodnight Mr Tom* when it was first screened, but I watched the repeat. It was a feel-good story that was extremely popular with the public and won John a BAFTA award. Typically, he took his young co-star up to the podium with him and paid tribute to his contribution to the programme's success. I found it poignant to watch because John was 'playing old' again – the beard helped – and I could not help thinking how sad it was that he will never really be that old.

He continued to enjoy success with *Kavanagh QC* and when it finished at the end of the fifth series in 1999, John began to look for new challenges. He played a doctor in a two-part story called *Plastic Man* in which his character had a family and home life as well. This was something of a departure for John, as was the torrid love affair at the heart of the story. It was something we had always hoped Morse would enjoy and it certainly set a few pulses racing.

In complete contrast, he then played Renard, a Catholic priest in occupied France and a character torn between the demands of his vocation and his hatred of the Nazis who are destroying his parishioners. Inner conflict was always John's forte. He could suggest suffering without having to speak, but he also had the most wonderful smile. When he used it, it lit up the screen.

For some years, no BAFTA awards ceremony had seemed complete without John picking up either the best actor award or the Lew Grade audience award.

The latter is highly valued by actors because it is the viewers who vote for it. In 1998, he was given the Lifetime Achievement Award in the National Television Awards and, in 2001, a BAFTA fellowship. This proved that his fellow professionals esteemed him as highly as the viewers did. Not bad for a lad from the back streets of Manchester who, with typical modesty, said that he just wanted to make people forget the gas bill for half an hour.

When I heard that John was ill, I was as upset as if he had been a close friend or even a member of my family. His appeal for privacy for himself and his family was typical. I knew his illness was serious and the lack of information over the months led me to fear the worst, but it was still a terrible shock when I heard the news of his death. I felt as if part of my youth went with him and I find it very hard to believe he has gone. The recent repeats of *Inspector Morse* and *The Sweeney* have served only to emphasise what a shining talent we have lost. Yet again, but in death, he won another BAFTA, for *Buried Treasure*, his last television play.

My dream career would have been to act, but I did not know if I had the talent and I did not have the courage to find out. Forty years ago it took a lot of courage and self-belief to follow that kind of dream and I am sure that there were many working class children like me who did not believe they could do it. John always said that acting was the only thing he could do, but it was not that simple. He had a miserable time in his first term at RADA and his share of lean times before the successes started. John was a complete professional who always gave 100 per cent, even in the occasional bits of fluff he appeared in. The awards and rewards he achieved were well deserved and somehow I always felt that he did it for all of us who did not have the courage to try.

A new kind of cop show

by Joseph Horodyski

A native of Stamford, Connecticut, Joseph Horodyski now lives in Ohio with his wife and two cats. He is a professional writer who has contributed extensively to *Newsweek* and *Popular Astronomy*. He also writes for American World War II history and military heritage magazines. He usually specialises in science and history, but has also written on local issues for *Stamford Advocate*, his hometown's newspaper. He has a series of detective short stories to his credit and is currently working on his first full-length novel. A John Thaw admirer for 'at least half my life', Joseph Horodyski is fascinated by the spread of Thaw's popularity to the United States and other countries across the world. His website http://johnthaw.topcities.com/johnthaw.html, which has won a Golden Web Award, is currently the only site devoted entirely to Thaw's life and career rather than to any specific television series.

On 2 January, 1975, a new kind of cop show – with a new kind of hero – burst on to British television screens. It was to change the face of television programming in England and to transform a relatively unknown actor into a national icon. The actor was John Thaw and the show was *The Sweeney.* In one of those wonderful accidents of fate, the show that was to launch John on a career – the likes of which he could hardly have imagined – premiered the day before his thirty-third birthday. John would soon have ample reason to celebrate both his birthday and the show's popularity with viewers.

The story of how *The Sweeney* came about is almost as interesting as the show itself. The mid-1970s were a relatively more civilised and innocent time in television action shows both in Britain and America. Most British viewers were being treated to imported American fare every night, but those police dramas that were then popular were starting to take on a grittier, harder edge – shows such as *SWAT*, *The Streets of San Francisco*, *Kojak* and *Starsky & Hutch*. Although almost fanciful in their portrayal of the life of an average cop, increasingly realistic heroes were beginning to show much more street wisdom. It reflected the changing times. Some of this new aware-ness was starting to make itself felt in British programmes as well. When British television set out to produce a home-grown product that would be the equal of anything created by its American cousins, it succeeded beyond its wildest expectations.

In the early 1970s, Thames Television formed a subsidiary company called Euston Films Ltd. to create and produce a line of 90-minute television dramas as part of its *Armchair Cinema* series. A full season of 13 programmes was originally conceived, but because of rising production costs – a then unheard of £85,000 per programme – only six were eventually completed: *The Prison*, *Regan*, *Sea Song*, *When Day Is Done*, *In Sickness and in Health* and *Tully*. Euston Films eventually recouped most of its investment by selling the broadcasting rights of these films to other countries. In the case of *The Prison* (no connection with *The Prisoner* starring Patrick McGoohan) and *Regan* that meant 47 different markets.

Regan was the brainchild of writer Ian Kennedy-Martin who had originally prepared it as a play. It was conceived in the mould of an earlier BBC police series, *Z Cars*, that had been created by his brother Troy. Euston Films was eager to make a programme in the American action-based style, and the company saw much potential in the unlikely hero of Jack Regan, a tough, no-nonsense, hard-drinking streetwise cop totally unlike anything British viewers had seen before. The American television network ABC-TV, which was then the dominant partner in Thames Television, gave the green light to the project and executives began looking for an actor to play Jack Regan.

Kennedy-Martin had worked with John Thaw a decade earlier when John had starred in his first television series, *Redcap*, with co-star Diana (now Dame Diana) Rigg in 1964–5. *Redcap* told the story of the Special Investigations Branch of the Royal Military Police investigating military crimes at various postings around the world. Although short lived, the series had given John Thaw some valuable experience in television work and was the first time he had been cast in the role of a policeman. Since then John had struck out, trying to establish himself in films and had made a few notable appearances. They ranged from the critically acclaimed *The Loneliness of the Long Distance Runner* to the abysmal shock-horror film *Dr Phibes Rises Again*. At the same time John was supplementing his income with appearances on television. Kennedy-Martin met John once more when Thaw guest-starred – again as a cop – on an episode of *Z Cars.* The two renewed their friendship and Kennedy-Martin never had any doubt that Thaw was exactly right for Jack Regan. After a brief screen test, John was immediately cast in the role.

Kennedy-Martin based the character of Jack Regan on a series of conversations with friends who were detectives from London's Flying Squad (a unit formed in the 1920s when they became the first police squad in Britain equipped with cars, later to be linked by radio, and thus able to respond instantly to any situation anywhere in the city). Kennedy-Martin's character reflected the attitude of men in the department who resented their new roles as desk clerks and paper pushers, endlessly filing reports and forms as a result of the bureaucracy that had crept into Scotland Yard's operations. They preferred being out on the streets among their contacts, meeting on darkened street corners or in dimly lit back rooms, constantly looking for ways to put underworld figures out of business. Kennedy-Martin envisioned a maverick cop who refused to play by the rules and bent every regulation in the book in a crusade to keep the streets clean of lowlife. When that series was later broadcast, some of The Sweeney's biggest fans were police officers that wished they could do exactly what their hero acted out on the small screen.

British Broadcasting Corporation 55 Paradise Street Liverpool L1 3BP Telephone 0151 708 5500 Fax 0151 794 0988/0151 794 0909 (News)
E-Mail radio.merseyside@bbc.co.uk Website www.bbc.co.uk/radiomerseyside or www.bbc.co.uk/liverpool

Radio Merseyside
Nations & Regions

Congratulations & Best Wishes

Angela Heslop .

With Compliments

Regan's creator gave him a wife, played by Janet Key, an airline stewardess who had walked out on her husband after years of neglect caused by his relentless pursuit of criminals on the mean streets of London. And, as every hero needs a sidekick, so Regan got sergeant George Hamilton Carter, a younger officer played by an old friend of John's, Dennis Waterman. Carter was meant to provide a restraining influence on Regan, always keeping him grounded in reality while they were engaged in crime-busting adventures. John and Dennis already knew each other and John had quickly become impressed with his younger friend's intense devotion to his craft. Their off-screen friendship would later enhance their on-screen work as Regan and Carter.

The writers pulled out all the stops for *Regan*. Superbly directed and with an intense performance by Thaw, it probably remains the best crime drama British television has ever produced. It is hard to imagine that there was ever any doubt that a series would follow. Unlike early episodes of *The Sweeney*, *Regan* focused exclusively on the main character, underlining his loner, almost maverick traits, as, isolated from his Scotland Yard colleagues, he embarks on a one-man vendetta to find the killers of a young policeman. The rest of the cast contributed outstanding performances – from Lee Montague's terrifying gangland boss (the scene involving an amputation with an ice skate's blade is both terrifying and breathtaking at the same time) to Maureen Lipman in a charming supporting role as Regan's girlfriend.

The two best scenes, however, are cleverly positioned next to one another. Regan has to visit the dead policeman's grandmother to break the unwelcome news to her. 'You know something?' he tells Carter as they sit outside her home in their car, rain softly falling on the glass, 'That old lady's got no reason to go on living anymore. Whoever killed Cowley really killed two people.' It is a beautiful scene made even more effective by being followed by one where Regan visits his ex-wife, Kate. As he tries to explain the reason why he's always late, she interrupts him, 'I'm not interested any more in your silly cases and your stupid criminals'. There is some superb black comedy, too, as Regan's tension distorts itself into an almost palpable offensiveness directed at his wife's new lover. Turning as it does seedy, violent, touching and exciting, *Regan* is a stunning piece of television.

Regan was first screened on Tuesday, 4 June,

1974 at 8.30 p.m. to respectable ratings, coming in third for the evening with an audience of seven million. It was always seen as a potential vehicle for a series. Producer Ted Childs, just embarking on what was to become a lifelong and productive friendship with John Thaw, immediately sold the idea to the studio for a series of 13 one-hour episodes. John and Dennis, who had developed a wonderful working rapport with each other, were both immediately signed on for the series. The project now became known as *The Sweeney* (the title being derived from the name *Sweeney Todd*, cockney rhyming slang for Flying Squad, which had been in use since the 1920s).

Building on the success of *Regan*, John's character was to be the focal point of the show. The format of weekly stories enabled Ted Childs to develop and expand the role. He gave Regan a background and character of some depth and armed with all the strengths, weaknesses, complex human traits and failings that you would expect to find in a realistic depiction of an individual intensely driven to succeed, whatever the cost. Detective Jack Regan was said to be 36. Like Thaw, he also came from Manchester. He was tough and resourceful, a four-year veteran of the Flying Squad whose single-minded commitment to the job had led to the breakdown of his marriage. He was divorced, but occasionally visited his eight-year old daughter. A consummate professional, Regan looked down on desk-bound bureaucrats and often dressed casually – against departmental regulations – as a private expression of protest within the squad. He was fond of women but not promiscuous. Although he often drank hard, he didn't let it interfere with his effectiveness at work. He was ruthless in pursuit of criminals and used whatever questionable methods it took to get the job done. Somewhat cynical in his outlook towards life, 'Don't bother me with filling out forms and following procedure,' became his motto. 'Just let me get out there and nick villains.'

John revelled in the challenge the role would bring him as an actor. He knew the part had the potential to turn him into a major star and was excited by the scripts. 'The great thing about the Flying Squad,' he once told an interviewer, 'is that it gets into almost every aspect of life where serious crime occurs and offers unlimited material with which to work. I perceive Regan as a cop who is precariously balanced between crime and the law. If he weren't such a very good cop, he would have made a very good crook. Policemen have got to be as cunning as the villains they are trying to catch. There's a lot of frustration in their job because the public sometimes doesn't give them the credit they deserve.' Were there any similarities between the character and the actor portraying him? 'In real life I'm not nearly as tough as Regan, but basically we're both pretty down-to-earth blokes. From that point of view, it was good casting.'

Sergeant George Carter was created as a 26-year old cockney, a good ten years younger than Regan, with a sharp wit and who admired his partner – even if they often disagreed over Regan's more aggressive approach to upholding the law. He always addressed Regan as 'Guv' in deference to his seniority. Detective Chief Inspector Frank Haskins, played by Garfield Morgan, provided the glue that held the department together. He was constantly quoting the rulebook to his subordinates whenever they crossed the line, which was quite frequently. The theme music, eventually to become one of the most recognisable in England during the 1970s, was a 40-second piece written by veteran composer Harry South.

To ensure accuracy and provide an air of authenticity to the show, Scotland Yard provided an adviser, former Flying Squad detective John Quarrie, to oversee the production from the standpoint of police procedures. This created a mixed result. It ensured accuracy with regard to police methods and terminology, but it also gave viewers the mistaken impression that Regan's drinking, womanising and break-all-the-rules attitude would also be acceptable in real life.

Writers were issued strict, formal guidelines to follow in the making of the show. A memo put out by the production company states 'Each show will have an overall screen time (minus titles) of 48 minutes and 40 seconds. Each film will open with a teaser of up to 3 minutes to be followed by the opening titles. The story will be played out across three acts, each act being no more than 19 minutes and no less than 8 minutes in length. Regan will appear in every episode, Carter in approximately 10 out of 13 episodes. In addition to these main characters, scripts should be based around three major speaking parts, with up to ten minor speaking parts.'

Each 3-minute 'teaser' was packed with as much action as possible. Shooting, punch-ups, squealing tyres or screeching brakes were all designed to hook viewers immediately and draw them in through a fast-moving montage of exciting, compelling images. It was precision programming at its best. Viewers and advertisers both knew just what they could expect from each week's episode. Once they were familiar with the story line and the backgrounds and personalities of the two leading men, the public just wanted more of the same, with of course, different plots and assorted villains each week. Kennedy-Martin himself would contribute two or three scripts per season.

Writers were given a month to write each script, but were often pushed to get them done as quickly as possible, which led to one episode being written in just three days. Second drafts of scripts were usually frowned upon, third drafts virtually unheard of. The filming of each episode normally took ten working days, shooting about five minutes of edited screen time per day. Because of this the number of different filming locations had to be restricted to ten, or one location per day.

There was a standing set built of the Flying Squad offices, which provided an alternative location should bad weather restrict a day's filming. Two days would normally be spent filming on the set, which meant that ten minutes of any given episode was set in the confines of the Squad's offices. Shooting also took place throughout the summer months during the long hours of daylight. Night shots were limited to about three minutes per episode. They were expensive to produce because the crews had to be paid overtime.

Each week's show had an eight and a half week production schedule. Two weeks were set aside for pre-production: casting the various roles called for in the script, finding shooting locations, etc. A further two weeks were used for filming. Picture editing took four weeks, the first two weeks of which would overlap with the shooting schedule in order to save valuable production time. Two weeks were allowed for sound editing and a further two and a half days for final dubbing.

Each episode was strictly budgeted at £40,000. The film crew had to be ready to move quickly to different locations, often at a moment's notice, but these were rarely more than an hour away from the main set at Colet Court, an abandoned school building in Hammersmith, West London, which served as Regan and Carter's Flying Squad offices.

Even though this hectic, demanding pace often needed John to work 16 hours days, he threw himself into the role with as much passion and drive as that of Jack Regan. This commitment gave Thaw's brilliant performance throughout the series a sense of depth and conviction seldom matched on television.

From the beginning, producer Ted Childs laid out a series of guidelines to be followed and set parameters for his team of writers working on *The Sweeney*. He wanted to create exciting, action-packed television that would hold viewers spellbound, while at the same time not exceeding the bounds of good taste. He stressed to his team, 'Major crime is often very violent and bloody, and one does not wish to flinch from the reality of this. Nonetheless, the series is being produced for transmission in both afternoon and evening family viewing hours. Accordingly, we must respect the rules laid down by the IBA [Independent Broadcasting Authority] with respect to language and dialogue and detailed descriptions of pathological forms of behaviour. Four-letter words are not permissible, nor can we indulge in offensive, 'souped-up' scenes of horror, such as representing, in slow motion, a security guard having his head blown off by a shotgun. We can cope with a limited number of fight scenes, car chases, shoot-outs, etc., but we cannot blow up literal representations of St Paul's nor bring the whole of Oxford Street to a grinding halt in order to wreck three police cars inside Selfridge's front window.'

The first *The Sweeney* was broadcast at 9.00 p.m. on Thursday, 2 January, 1975. An estimated five million viewers saw this episode, 'Ringer'. During the opening minutes, the show quickly set the style with Regan hurling a suspect up against a wall, seizing him by the throat and snarling, 'We're the Sweeney son, so if you don't want a kickin' ...' It was brash, compelling and so unexpected that it made for electrifying television. Interestingly, Thames Television did not quite know what to make of its new creation. 'Ringer' had not been released in advance to the press for review because corporate executives were fearful of negative reactions regarding the level of violence. A much tamer episode, 'Thin Ice' (the third actually broadcast) was presented to them instead.

The *Daily Telegraph* was lavish in its praise of the opening episode. Television critic Richard Last wrote that the studio had created a 'very superior police thriller in *The Sweeney.* I doubt very much if Scotland Yard will relish a new TV detective inspector whose idea of interrogation is to force the suspect up against a wall and massage his head a bit. Yet, as portrayed by John Thaw and the deceptively innocent-looking Dennis Waterman, both characters are entirely believable, a world away from the cardboard cut-out characters of most ITV police serials.'

A few outstanding episodes quickly set the pace for

the shows that were to follow. In 'Stoppo Driver', after a criminal gang's driver is killed in a high-speed car chase, the villains urgently need to recruit a new 'chauffeur' for their underworld operations. Who better than a highly-skilled member of the Flying Squad itself – who turns out to be Regan and Carter's own new driver.

In 'Night Out', a Kennedy-Martin story, the Flying Squad is informed of a planned bank raid and is desperately trying to locate the gang's lookout man. It turns out that the equipment the crooks are planning to use to gain entrance into the tightly-sealed vault is being smuggled over London rooftops through the flat of one of Regan's many old flames. Haskins, Regan's superior, sees a golden opportunity to grab some publicity by making a clean sweep of the gang. He assigns Regan to spend a night out with her.

'Contact Breaker' also finds Regan and Carter at the scene of a bank raid. The bank manager tells them that there appears to have been insider knowledge. The evidence points to a recently released convict on probation, but Regan and Carter have doubts. It turns out that evidence had been planted to lead the cops away from the actual mastermind, a member of the Flying Squad's own ranks.

In the season's final episode, 'Abduction', Regan's own eight-year old daughter, Susie, is kidnapped. This stunning episode features one of John Thaw's best performances as a man on the edge who will stop at nothing to save the life of his child.

The series maintained respectable ratings throughout all 13 episodes. The highest-rated show came second for the week in which it was shown, with 8.75 million viewers. Thaw won glowing reviews from critics for the way he effectively portrayed Regan's bitter, world-weary attitude towards the often dirty, thankless job he had to do. 'I sometimes hate this bastard place,' Regan states in one scene, 'It is a bloody holiday camp for thieves and weirdoes, all the rubbish. You find yourself ageing prematurely, trying to sort some of it out. You try your best to protect the public and all they do is call you a fascist for it. You nail a villain and some ponced-up, pinstriped barrister screws you up like an old fag packet on a point of procedure, then pops off for a game of squash and a glass of Madeira. He's taking home 30 grand a year and we can just about afford ten days in Eastbourne and a second-hand car.'

Cars became a very popular part of The Sweeney's appeal. The 1970s was not a very auspicious time for the British motor industry and this point was re-inforced by Regan choosing to use a brown Ford Granada (registration NKH 295 M). He never drove himself, but would laze laconically in the front or back seat. He never wore a seat belt. Occasionally a blue Ford Cortina (registration NKH 296 M) would appear whenever Regan and Carter had to split into two separate teams to accomplish a job, or when a back-up vehicle was needed, but Regan never considered it as flashy as his Granada. These two vehicles quickly became the stars of the opening credits. The villains, however, almost always drove a Jaguar Mark II or sometimes an 'S' model. The powerful engine made for quick getaways and added a touch of class that helped elevate the status of the villain-of-the-week above that of a mere petty burglar. They often gave Regan a run for his money, but on account of their vehicles' 'soggy' suspension and chronic unreliability our heroes usually got the upper hand in the end.

John learned much in the unforgiving classroom of a weekly series. For example, he discovered how easily the handling of props could cause problems with continuity. 'Don't smoke in a scene if you can help it,' he said for example. 'Hold the bloody thing in your hand but for goodness sake don't smoke it. If you have to do six or seven takes, you'll end up green in the face. Later on, when I played Morse, who hap-pened to drink gallons of real ale, that precious bit of experience was vital as you might guess. Luckily, I don't like beer much. But anyway, you must take the pint glass, be careful to take just a sip or two and then put it down. But don't ever touch it again during the scene. It makes life so much easier.'

The Sweeney's second season began on 1 Sept-ember, 1975 on a new night, Monday. Two episodes rocketed to number one in the ratings, with one episode, 'Country Boy', achieving 8.8 million viewers, the largest audience of the season. Carter's wife, played by Stephanie Turner, had been killed off, which enabled the show to focus more on the police work with attractive guest stars as various 'girlfriends of the week'. The dynamic duo now spent more time together eyeing up the birds, supporting each other when their romantic involvements inevitably founder-ed and studying life through the bottoms of their beer glasses.

Episodes continued to be of high quality. In 'Faces', after three payroll robberies in two days, the duo suspected a local German thug, working for a right-wing terrorist organisation. They set up an ambush to catch the crooks but it failed miserably. Soon it is obvious there is an informer in the squad.

Often the series' edgy, hard-hitting action was topped off with a sly, counterbalancing sense of humour, which served as a welcome break from the tension of that week's story. At one point, Regan menacingly informs a suspect, 'We're the Sweeney, son, and we haven't had our dinner yet, so be careful'. In another, asked if he drank while on duty, Regan snaps back, 'Only whisky'. Introducing his partner Carter to a colleague, Regan declares, 'This is my sergeant. He hits people for a living.' Audiences across Britain loved it.

The Sweeney also introduced a whole new vocabulary. Regan and Carter continually mixed with some of London's seedier personalities as a way of making contacts in the criminal underworld. Armed robbers became blaggers, money was readies and informants were transformed into snouts. Other popular phrases were bird for time in prison, Bob Hope for drugs, brass for a prostitute, brown bread for dead and froth and bubble for trouble (sometimes wife-related). Gasmeter thieves became a derisive term for minor crooks, Jacks for five-pound notes, doing a Royal meant turning Queen's evidence, a fit-up was false evidence and weighed-in meant paying a debt. Indeed, because so many such expressions were used in the scripts, some local newspapers printed glossaries.

There were special, favourite lines that the writers would try to include as often as possible. 'Get yer trousers on, you're nicked,' became a catch phrase whenever a criminal was arrested and 'Shut it' became a highly-popular replacement for 'keep quiet'. This London-flavoured dialogue was delivered convincingly enough for Thaw to be regularly asked which part of the capital city he came from. Many reviewers were surprised to learn of his Manchester origins.

The show's quick acceptance by the viewing public convinced the producers that they were on to something lucrative. But how best to exploit it? During filming of the second season's episodes, they quickly decided to make a film based on the highly-rated show, which was very unusual. Thames Television put up most of the £1.4 million budget and EMI Studios provided the rest. Nat Cohen, EMI's boss, was an admirer of *The Sweeney* on television, but, before putting up any money, he wanted to know what extra attractions a film would have to persuade television viewers to part with a few extra pounds at the cinema. Ted Childs later remembered that he had no ready answer. All he had was a gut feeling that it would work. Luckily, Cohen had enough faith in Childs to back the project. Apart from the financial contribution, EMI's agreement to become a partner in the venture would also turn out to be crucial when it came to distributing the film. It ensured that it would be guaranteed the widest UK release possible through the chain of ABC cinemas that were then owned and operated by EMI.

Everyone was under pressure to make a film that would attract audiences, not just in Britain but also around the world, especially in the lucrative American market. *The Sweeney* was, by now, an international sensation in over 40 different countries. It was popular in such diverse places as Argentina, Australia, Canada, Peru, Spain and even Swaziland. In Canada, viewers even asked the director of programming for CTV to provide subtitles to help them understand the cockney rhyming slang.

Shot on location in London over a period of five weeks during the spring of 1976, *Sweeney!* the 90-minute film, was released in early 1977. The reviews were mixed. Censorship standards had been relaxed to meet the more liberal regulations dealing with cinema films. As a result, many more of the potentially offensive four-letter words were used in the film than in the more stringently controlled television version of the show.

The plot involved Regan and Carter investigating a suicide, in the process, uncovering a conspiracy involving government MPs and big businessmen, namely oil barons. They would stop at nothing to achieve their sinister aims of strangling the world's economy through control of its oil.

Directed by David Wickes and written by Ronald Graham, the film opens with an intentional act of self-parody. Regan and Carter are shown waking up late and drunk alongside air stewardesses. Barry Foster convincingly played a blackmailing personal secretary to a government minister who also excelled at extortion, prostitution and murder. Ian Bannen shone in his role as the MP. The film is full of shadowy hit men, usually armed with submachine guns and explosives, often impersonating police officers as a way of gaining access to their intended victims. The plot involves enough car chases and shoot-outs to put even the series to shame, including the machine-gunning of three villains in broad daylight in a scrapyard, a hit man posing as a window cleaner who plants a bomb in the offices of a newspaper reporter, and the shooting-up of a hotel room from gangsters positioned outside on the fire escape. Carter ends up blaming Regan for the death of the Barry Foster character in a controversial freeze-frame ending intended to leave viewers expecting a sequel.

Loyal fans of the television series turned the film into a box-office success and it was quickly sold overseas in numerous markets, including, much to the producer's own surprise, China. It thus achieved a notable footnote in history by becoming the first Western film ever to be shown in that communist country.

John Thaw and Dennis Waterman basked in their new-found success on the big screen. Even though some critics condemned it as mindless violence, the public ate it up. The two leading men cut contrasting figures. John with his already greying hair and Dennis tall, thin and with obvious movie star good looks. Dennis is an extrovert while John was almost painfully shy. They performed many of their own stunts both on the show and in the film. Each man perfectly complemented the other's acting style. 'I was very lucky in *The Sweeney* to strike up a great partnership with Dennis,' John once said. 'We got on very well together and I think that showed on-screen.' John found Dennis's cheerful attitude on the set contagious. Thaw tended to take his work extremely seriously and to exercise strict self-discipline, but on *The Sweeney* Dennis was able to teach him how to relax and find humour in his work. 'I can share a joke now during work as well as off the set, which I'd never been able to do before,' Thaw confessed.

In return, working with such a highly respected professional as John Thaw boosted Waterman's own self-confidence. 'Through John's discipline and strength, I've learned to calm down and be more in control,' he confided during one interview. Dennis was always grateful for the lasting friendship that developed between him and his popular co-star. 'When the series started in 1975, I was just one of the coppers in the squad. But John kept pushing me into more things. He'd say to the directors "Give this scene to Dennis. Give him another close-up". It was John's idea to develop us into a sort of double-act. He could have grabbed all the attention for himself, but he didn't.' It was a trait to which anyone who worked with John Thaw throughout his remarkable career could attest.

The Sweeney's third season began on 6 September, 1976 with the critically acclaimed 'Selected Target.' Again, *The Sweeney* reached number one in the ratings with its first episode. Later in the season it gained its largest audience with 9.4 million viewers in the UK. But by this time *The Sweeney* was also coming under increasing fire for its violent content and 'foul' language, as Thames Television had originally feared that it might.

Television executives did not have to wait long before protests began. Some of Britain's highest-ranking policemen apparently did not approve of the image it created in the public's mind. Sir David McNee, the then Metropolitan Police Commissioner, criticised *The Sweeney's* influence by saying, 'For a policeman to carry out his duties by following the example set by *The Sweeney* would be setting out on the road to disaster'. Thaw found himself more and more frequently having to defend the show and he chose to speak out on several occasions, declaring how much he detested violence. 'I hate it. But I believe that there is no gratuitous violence in the series. What there is comes out of the situations the characters find themselves in. After all, we're trying to get some sense of realism. By the very nature of their job, Flying Squad boys have got to be tough. Regan never gets aggressive with anyone who doesn't deserve it.'

Thaw was so convincing as Regan and the two men became so identified with one another in viewers' minds, that his wife, Sheila, was more than once forced to explain that, despite the menacing image her husband projected on television, he was nothing like that at home. 'He frightens me sometimes when I watch him on the show. He looks so aggressive, but he's really a big softie inside. He works so hard at getting bruised and battered for the sake of his craft that it's often a pale shadow of a man who comes home every night, not exactly a roaring lion bashing down the door.'

Controversy was never distant and criticism came from all around. The National Viewers' and Listeners' Association deplored the bad language and violence which, it said, the show glamorised. 'Police officers are not, as a matter of course, foul-mouthed, sadistically violent or promiscuous they argued, and once claimed there had been 37 incidents of 'foul or coarse' language in a single episode. The truth was quite different. It was an illusion. By breaking ground in its use of common street language, the show was skilfully able to create an impression in viewers' minds that far more of such language was being used than they were really hearing.

An examination of the shows, now that they are

available on video, reveals that the words which so offend some people occur three or four times per programme – about once per act – and it's usually not much more than referring to someone as a bastard or son-of-a-bitch. The complaints reached a climax in an episode titled 'May' from the third series. It contained seven 'unacceptable' expressions, far fewer than was usually claimed by self-appointed watchdogs such as Mary Whitehouse of The National Viewers and Listeners' Association. Some of the more memorable lines they objected to, mild by today's standards, included Regan's 'I am utterly and abjectly pissed off' or his more colourful, 'If you weren't who you are I'd kick your arse up to your shoulder blades'.

Much more unexpected, however, was an attack on the series based on a survey of London teenagers conducted by Dr William Belson, a psychiatrist, who found that 'Young boys exposed to high levels of TV violence were much more likely to commit serious crimes in their lives'. Ted Childs swiftly countered by pointing out, accurately, that the majority of the show's fans were over the age of 60. 'If our critics had been right,' he argued, 'shopping precincts would have been full of marauding, gun-toting, senior citizens beating the rest of us over our heads with their pension books.' It was an old debate and one that will remain with us long after The Sweeney becomes a mere footnote in television history.

Chief Inspector John Robinson, lecturing on investigative procedures at the Police Training School in Hendon, publicly complained that the show revealed too much secret information about police methods. Commenting on Thaw's portrayal of Jack Regan, he argued that, 'Regan hands out closely guarded trade secrets as if they were on special offer at your local supermarket. Crime is a very costly and serious business, not a game. Yet here is a show handing out secrets absolutely free of charge. There is not a young copper who could not learn a thing or two from watching the programme so imagine what it must do for the villains. They probably welcome it with open arms.'

Former Flying Squad supervisor, Frank Davies, added his thoughts. 'The Sweeney is an insult to a small group of extremely devoted, highly professional officers respected throughout the world. No policeman keeping watch during a bank raid would spend his time jumping in and out of a woman's bed. As for all the violent, senseless shootings in the show and some very far-fetched scenes, especially one that depicted an officially sanctioned kidnapping, this is pure rubbish and the very height of fantasy. The sex scenes needlessly worry the wives and girlfriends of decent, respectable officers. They give a false image of life within the Squad. But many neighbours and friends think it's a true reflection because of what they see on the screen each week.' Davies finished his outspoken tirade to the press by insisting that there should be a preface to the show insisting that each episode was a work of fiction.

Nevertheless, not everyone was alarmed by *The Sweeney*. Several Scotland Yard detectives privately let it be known to Thames Television that they weren't offended by being portrayed as tough and uncompromising. In fact, they rather liked the idea. John Thaw was even presented with an engraved silver cigarette case by the Battersea detectives that proclaimed, 'We wish all DIs [detective inspectors] were like you'. More importantly for Thames Television, however, was the fact that the public loved the show. To combat critics who were beginning to think that *The Sweeney* was getting stale, Euston Films quickly began production on a second feature film based on the series.

Released in March 1978, the 108-minute *Sweeney II* followed the tried-and-tested formula laid down in the series by mixing thrilling action with dark humour.

Tom Clegg directed it and Troy Kennedy-Martin, Ian's brother, scripted it. Location filming took place in London and on Malta. The film has many non-politically correct moments as the heroes pursue a sophisticated gang of bank robbers. One comic scene involves the bomb squad, along with Regan and Carter, drinking in a hotel while an explosive device is being defused in an adjoining room. If this really happened, it would dominate newspaper front pages for days. John Thaw and Dennis Waterman repeated their impressive double-act and the film outdid its predecessor, especially towards the end when the shootings, explosions and consequent body count gets out of hand.

The supporting cast within the television series featured some familiar faces, including Denholm Elliott as a corrupt ex-chief inspector, Patrick Malahide as Major Conway and the late, ever-classy Nigel Hawthorne as Dilke. Indeed, a large number of British film and television veterans delightedly relished a chance to appear in the series. A long line of guest-stars who passed through the show includes Brian Blessed, John Clive, Brian Glover, Derrick O' Connor, John Hurt, and Roy Kinnear.

The Sweeney's lasting popularity produced a whole

range of merchandise tie-ins to the programme. Omnia Pastimes, for example, produced a *The Sweeney* board game, in 1975. The object was for four players to work in teams of two, with two teams being villains and the other two being *The Sweeney.* The aim is for a player to meet up with his partner at randomly designated places on the board to conduct a 'raid'. After a successful raid on a location, points are awarded and added to a scoreboard. The winner is the first up the scoreboard to number 14. Today, the game can fetch a lot of money at auctions. A short-lived series of trading cards also followed.

Also popular were the inevitable tie-in novels, the first of which was written by Ian Kennedy-Martin himself and has now become a much sought-after collector's item. In the rush to publish the paperback in order to take advantage of the growing wave of popularity, the publishers, Futura Press, committed the huge error of misspelling the title in large bold letters on the cover as '*Sweeny'* without the third e. This mistake has made that first edition the most highly prized of all the books. At least six other titles were released in 1977 during the height of 'Sweeneymania'. These provocative-sounding publications were *Regan and The Manhatten File, Regan and the Deal Of The Century, Regan and The Lebanese Shipment, Regan and The Human Pipeline, Regan and The Snout Who Cried Wolf* and the curious-sounding *Regan and The Bent Stripper.*

Let us not forget *The Sweeney's* contribution to modern style. Regan's trademark was a crumpled sheepskin coat. He lived in a flat with early eight-track tape decks, an electric fire, nail-and-string pictures, plastic potted plants, fibre optic lamps, velvet artwork, and cheap gold sunburst-style wall clocks and other 1970s 'mod' statements. Those who wanted to could decorate their home as if it, too, had raided a charity shop for 1970s items.

By the end of *The Sweeney's* third series, John was beginning to feel that he had taken the character of Jack Regan as far as it could go and that he could get little more out of the role. Then he discovered that Dennis Waterman felt the same. So the two stars gathered the production team together to reassess the show. John eventually suggested that they should all treat the forthcoming fourth series as if it were their first. All concerned threw themselves into their work with a renewed vigour.

The Sweeney's fourth series began on 7 September, 1978, returning to its original Thursday evening time. The scripts were consistently good and the writers managed to inject the series with some of the flavour of the Hollywood box-office blockbuster *The French Connection*. Reviewers often found the stars' performances so convincing and natural that some even wondered whether the dialogue had been ad-libbed by the actors rather than scripted. *The Sweeney* successfully carried John Thaw to the height of television ratings time and again. By now, the show had become such a staple among viewers' weekly schedules that the lowest audience for its fourth season was an astounding 10.9 million – far higher than the highest-rated episode of any previous season. It was also during its fourth year that the show reached the pinnacle of its success with 19.5 million viewers for a repeat episode entitled 'Selected Target'. That was achieved four days before Christmas 1978 and was more than double any previous viewing audience.

To his astonishment, John Thaw soon found that *The Sweeney* had turned him into not only a national star, but also a sex symbol. Admiring letters arrived regularly at Thames Television's studios from female viewers across the country. During the first series, over 150 Bunnies at London's Playboy Club in Park Lane had voted John to the top of their Bunnies' Valentine's Day poll. John's reward, in addition to being the Bunnies' top pin-up, would have been a kiss and honorary membership of the prestigious London club. He tactfully turned down the offer through his agent who explained that it wasn't quite John's style.

John's following grew during *The Sweeney* years, but he also endured a tiresome phase of being identified with Jack Regan, which he hated mostly because of what he termed its 'nuisance value'. Complete strangers often unexpectedly wound down their car windows to mutter something about Regan to him. It was one of the inevitable drawbacks of stardom to be recognised and pointed at almost everywhere he went in public. Once, he discovered a young girl camped outside his Chiswick home. A devoted fan, she had journeyed all the way from Nottingham in the hope of catching a fleeting glimpse of her idol. John had no idea she was there until his unexpected admirer knocked on his door at seven in the morning one winter's day. Always a gentleman, Thaw invited her in and made her a steaming cup of coffee to help warm her up. She later happily went on her way, thrilled at having met the object of her affections. Immediately, she took it upon herself to start circulating news to other *Sweeney* fans about what the actor was really like.

During the filming of the fourth series, both stars felt that *The Sweeney* had reached the end of the road. Despite pleas and substantial financial inducements from Thames Television who wanted the show to continue for at least another two series, Thaw and Waterman wanted to quit while they were ahead. The studio broke the news that they were calling it a day while John was on location, filming some scenes in Kilburn.

It was a bold move. John later confessed that the price he and Dennis were paying for their much-deserved success was just too high to maintain much longer. It was beginning to affect their families adversely because the long-running series had become a burden on their home lives. 'I'm like a real-life policeman, never knowing from day to day what time I am going to get in,' Thaw complained. 'And when you do get home, you're too tired to be good company to anyone. You rarely get to see your friends and family any longer when you're at your best.'

John would sometimes leave to begin shooting an average day's work at six in the morning and not return home until after ten at night. 'Domestically it created a lot of problems,' John explained. 'You'd leave your house at the crack of dawn not knowing what time you'd be able to get back home. Occasionally, I'd pass my wife on the stairs and that might be the total of our contact for an entire week. Since we often filmed for up to six months at a time, I finally decided that enough was enough. I knew it was time to get my priorities right.'

John also approached the decision from the standpoint of his craft as an actor. 'I was very frightened of going stale. The series started out marvellously enough in the beginning and this latest batch is among the best we've ever done, in my opinion. But we want to move on while we are winning.' Waterman shared Thaw's sentiments. 'As actors you just can't go on doing the same thing year after year indefinitely. But we're going to miss each other very much. John and I have had a tremendous working relationship ever since we first started and we've been personal friends off-screen too.'

As a treat for their many loyal fans, in November 1978, viewers got to see Eric Morecambe and Ernie Wise, Britain's most outstanding comedy act of their day, making a special guest appearance in the episode 'Hearts and Minds'. They played themselves as a pair of innocent bystanders who became caught up in a case that revolved around a missing college professor and blackmail. Morecambe and Wise had invited John and Dennis to guest star on their own Christmas television special some two years before. An invitation to appear on what many considered the funniest television show Britain had ever produced was widely regarded as the highest accolade that an actor could achieve. Thaw and Waterman were elated to get the call and agreed to appear on condition that the comic duo would return the compliment and appear on *The Sweeney.*

The final episode, 'Jack or Knave', was written by producer Ted Childs and went out on 28 December, 1978, barely a week before John's thirty-seventh birthday. It began with a brutal, bloody robbery and, despite a judge's commendation for his work in solving the case, Regan found himself arrested on suspicion of accepting bribes some ten years earlier. He was unceremoniously thrown into a cell like a common criminal before being cleared of charges in time for the show's dramatic conclusion. Regan emerged into the daylight, not unnaturally extremely cynical and bitter at the experience. This enabled John Thaw the actor to bow out as compulsively watchable as when

Jack Regan had first arrived on-screen two films and 53 episodes before. It was a foretaste of things to come when viewers of *Inspector Morse* were kept wondering about their beloved character's Christian name until almost the end of the final series. In *The Sweeney's* final episode, during his arrest, Regan's full name – John Albert Regan – was declared for the first time.

'I'm utterly pissed off with this lot,' was Thaw's final line of the series. 'I've given the best years of my life to this bloody job. I've got 18 commendations and how does this wonderful police force of ours show its gratitude for all my years of unstinting effort? It bangs me up in a cruddy little cell. I'm going to have to be reinstated and what do you bunch of gleaming, double-eyed hookheads do now? You want me to crawl back to work and be very grateful that I didn't get nicked for something that I didn't do in the first place. Well, you can stuff it.' And with that, Regan and *The Sweeney* vanished from the screen and into television history.

Once the decision to end *The Sweeney* had been taken, John couldn't make his exit quickly enough. Only a week after filming his final scenes as Jack Regan, Thaw was hard at work looking for new and exciting roles that were as far removed from his most famous alter ego as it was possible for him to get. He longed to put Regan behind him and tackle new roles in his career that would help challenge him further as an actor. Yet *The Sweeney* never fully left him, much as – to an even greater degree – the role of Morse refused to. Eventually, John came to terms with it. The show had made him a household name, familiar to millions of television viewers, and gave him the artistic freedom to pick and choose his next projects with a new confidence.

The show's final episode left open the remote possibility of John and Dennis resurrecting their roles at some distant point in the future. From time to time over the next five years, John would receive invitations to lunch with the producers of the show. Always hopeful of reviving *The Sweeney* magic, they sounded out John as to whether he ever saw himself returning to the role of Jack Regan. But proud as he was of his accomplishments in the series and grateful for the recognition it gained for him, Thaw always made it clear that he had moved on.

In 1983, however, he surprised everyone by announcing that he had changed his mind and was now considering a return to the role that had made him famous. This change of heart was the result of a conversation with a top-ranking police official who asked John when *The Sweeney* would be returning. He said how much he and many of his colleagues on the force had enjoyed the show and added that, since John was an actor, why didn't he just give his fans what they longed for? After all, it was they who paid his salary in the first place. John went home that night and found it difficult to sleep. His thoughts were filled with all the reasons why he had said he would never again step into Regan's shoes. 'I came to the conclusion that there was no reason in the world why I shouldn't do it,' he explained. 'I could do a film instead of a series. After all, it would only be six weeks out of my life, not six months.'

John even went to the trouble of consulting Dennis Waterman to find out whether he would agree to team up again. Although they both felt that another television series was definitely out of the question, it became conceivable that Regan and Carter could reunite in a feature film. 'Talking to that policeman reminded me that, dare I say it, *The Sweeney* was a well-made product. It had the appearance of reality, it was entertaining and people seemed to enjoy it.'

But the return of Regan and Carter never materialised. By then, John Thaw and Dennis Waterman were both too committed to other projects. Thaw was put out when Thames Television announced plans in early 1991 to show the original television-movie *Regan* when he was beginning to promote his latest television venture *Stanley and the Women*. Although John had granted Thames permission to screen several episodes of *The Sweeney* in 1990, he felt that this proposal was a transparent attempt to cash in on the film's enduring popularity before Thames Television lost its lucrative ITV franchise. He labelled the studio's decision a disgrace. In an angry statement released to the press, John stated that, 'They should be busy making new shows, not putting out a 17-year-old film which will end up costing them just a few hundred pounds to show. It's unforgivable.'

It is often said that imitation is the sincerest form of flattery and, in the quarter century since *The Sweeney* left the small screen, much homage has been paid to it. The series has remained in viewers' memories to such an extent that, in 1997, Nissan based an entire advertising campaign for its *Almera* model on *The Sweeney*. Two television commercials featured a bickering duo looking very much like Regan and Carter while driving their newly acquired *Almera* on the trail of some slippery crooks (even though in the television series the detectives were never allowed to drive themselves, but were always assigned a departmental driver). It was considered to be such a novelty that the commercials were unveiled amid much fanfare at the Prince Charles Theatre in London's fashionable West End. The outside of the theatre was bathed in flashing blue light and swathed in official-looking tape proclaiming 'Police line – do not cross' while two Nissan *Almeras* were parked Sweeney-style. There even appeared a clever print advertisement spoofing *The Sweeney* with a Regan-style cop leaping from his car and bellowing the famous 'Shut it!' to anyone who dared utter a word.

The popular *Harry Hill* show on Channel 4, filmed at Teddington Studios, the former home of Thames Television, introduced us each week to his little son Alan Hill who, for reasons unknown, enters on stage to the catchy *The Sweeney* theme music. There also existed in 1994 a short-lived punk rock group calling itself 'Carter, The Unstoppable Sex Machine', with one video showing members of the band driving around in a *Sweeney*-styled car while another member sits in a police interview room awaiting 'questioning'. This video was cleverly intercut with scenes from the movie

Sweeney II. One of the band's releases was a number called 'Regan & Carter Mix.'

For the last few years a pop group in Essex called *The Sweeney* has been making waves. It opens every show with the popular catch-phrase 'We're the Sweeney. Get yer trousers on, you're nicked.'

In 1982 and again in 1993, *The Sweeney* was parodied in the 'humour' magazine *The Comic Strip*, with the later version, *Detectives on the Edge of a Nervous Breakdown* featuring a plot where a number of famous television detectives were being killed off by an unknown serial killer. Jasper Carrot and Robert Powell created a series of *Sweeney* spoofs that originated as a comic sketch in one of Carrot's BBC monologue shows. It, too, included some all-too-familiar theme music. And, perhaps inspired by America's popular reality-based television show *Cops,* in 1989 Thames Television made a you-are-there kind of series called *The Flying Squad*, which was meant to show that the real-life London crime busters were not at all like the characters shown in *The Sweeney.*

Finally, Channel 4's once popular daily television soap drama, *Brookside,* set in and around a Liverpool housing development and broadcast since 1982, features a shop selling second-hand goods called *The Sweeney*. *The Sweeney's* influences continue to resonate a quarter of a century after it ended.

In 1999, plans were underway for a remake of *The Sweeney.* The creative vision once again came from the show's architect, Ian Kennedy-Martin. Dennis Waterman was all set to revive his role as George Carter, now promoted to the position of senior officer in the Flying Squad. As John Thaw had turned down an offer to make occasional guest appearances, the character of Jack Regan was to have been written out of the story as having retired to run a salmon farm in the north of Scotland. Now that Thaw has died, however, it seems unlikely that this will come to anything because of his powerful and permanent association with *The Sweeney* in the minds of the public.

Today, however, *The Sweeney* is enjoying a new lease of life, thanks in large part to Granada Television's decision to show all 53 episodes on weekday evenings, and the release of *Regan*, both *Sweeney* movies and a selection of *The Sweeney* episodes on video and DVD. A new audience, as well as a hard core of original, devoted and loyal fans have thrilled to the opportunity to watch the shows the second time round. *Sweeney* lingo is in vogue again, along with a new appreciation of the shows and its stars. An entire new generation of young viewers, some of whom were not even alive when the programmes were made, has enjoyed becoming *The Sweeney* connoisseurs. Such is the legacy of *The Sweeney.*

What of John Thaw, the man the show transformed from a struggling actor into a national icon? Did the show set him on the path to greatness, or forever typecast him in the role of a policeman? Even though further greatness and worldwide stardom awaited him in the remaining 14 years of his life, it is beyond doubt that the show helped John further hone his craft and acting style.

The significance of *The Sweeney's* place in the history of British television cannot be underestimated. Indeed, prominent media figure Jeremy Isaacs once described the show as 'One of the most successful series ever produced for British television. It took on Hollywood at its own game and played to win.' *The Sweeney* overtook the much-heralded American cop shows popular in the 1970s and relegated them to second-place status. It provided ITV with a solid, reliable product and a guaranteed prime-time ratings winner, becoming in the process a highly-acclaimed

model for the next generation of television producers to follow.

John Thaw's contribution to the show's success was inestimable, indeed, he *was* the show. Without question, he made Jack Regan the most famous television cop of the 1970s. His powerful, unerring performance carried with it that priceless asset of appealing to both men and women of all ages. *The Sweeney* was constantly setting new standards of realism for exciting fights, believable characters, dramatic car chases and sparkling dialogue. During that decade, there was no better or more popular television copper to be found anywhere. Indeed, successful shows, such as today's *NYPD Blue* , owe much to the likes of *The Sweeney* which paved the way for such shows in both style and content.

Today, John Thaw's television techniques are much admired and studied by his fellow actors and many rising stars. *The Sweeney* was John Thaw's life for four years and one might speculate how his career might have followed a very different path if Ted Childs had not offered him the role of Jack Regan in 1974. For example, when the offer came, John was starring in a highly praised situation comedy called *Thick As Thieves* , which co-starred Bob Hoskins as Dobbs, a petty crook who had been released from jail only to find that his best friend Stan, played by Thaw, had moved in with his wife Annie. The six-part series was highly regarded by critics and viewers alike and the show's producers wanted to develop it further, possibly by sending the two men back to prison. Although studio executives initially liked the idea, they hesitated about going ahead with the project because they feared the clever writing might go over the heads of an ITV audience. Their indecision meant that John was free to take up Ted Childs's offer to star in *Regan*, and the rest, as they say, is history. From such chances are stars made.

Thaw's film career never quite got off the ground. Television was his medium. In it, he found a wealth of dramatic material that not only kept him busy for the rest of his life, but also earned him a place in the hearts of the public and the recognition of his peers. Such rewarding personal satisfaction was all John Thaw really craved. He reaped its rewards in abundance.

Stranded on a musical island

by Susan Elkin

An invitation to spend half an hour on the BBC's imaginary island, chatting to Sue Lawley about the music necessary to while away the boredom beneath the palm trees, is a sure sign of arrival for actors, writers, politicians and other people in the public eye in Britain. John Thaw's turn came on 9 October, 1990 when he was 48 years old. *The Sweeney* was history. *Inspector Morse* was well established. *Kavanagh QC*, *Goodnight Mr Tom*, *Plastic Man* and the rest lay in the future. So did his 1993 CBE (Commander of the Order of the British Empire). Thaw's *Desert Island Discs* was quite an unusual opportunity for his, by then adoring, public to hear him speaking as and for himself rather than in any kind of role. It was an aural glimpse of the man behind that well-known 'lived-in' face.

Desert Island Discs, which was first broadcast in 1942, is one of BBC Radio's longest-running weekly programmes. It was the brainchild of Roy Plomley who presented it for 43 years until his death in 1985. Each guest is asked to imagine that he or she is stranded – probably permanently – on some remote tropical ocean islet. The only sources of comfort there are eight records (and the means to play them), an inanimate luxury and one book to add to the Bible and Shakespeare that are fortuitously lying about on the shore. Using discussion of their life and work as a backdrop, 'castaways' explain their choice of records, book and luxury to the presenter. Sue Lawley has been the voice of *Desert Island Discs* since 1988.

The cerebral, quiet Thaw, it turned out, was a lot closer to Morse in his musical and cultural tastes than he was to the earthy muscularity of Jack Regan. 'My love of classical music began when I was at RADA [Royal Academy of Dramatic Art],' he told Lawley, having first discussed with her his single parent family background in a Manchester council flat and his pre-RADA work in the local fruit and vegetable market. 'I shared a flat for a while with fellow RADA student Tom Courtenay who was very knowledgeable about classical music and introduced me to it.'

The breakthrough piece was Sibelius' Fifth Symphony – the first record played on the programme. Thaw was playing Mephistopheles in a student production of Goethe's *Faust* and becoming anxious about the role and his ability to identify with it. Courtenay advised him to listen to the Sibelius which he thought might help his friend and flatmate to work out something in the Mephistopheles persona. 'I was sceptical at first, but the moment I heard that music, I was transfixed and everything fell into place,' Thaw recalled.

Before then, Thaw was a man who knew only the sort of popular classics he might hear on *Family Favourites* on the radio, such as a snatch of Elgar's *Enigma Variations* or Kathleen Ferrier singing an aria. His father was a long distance lorry driver, obliged to raise Thaw and his younger brother Raymond on his own after their mother had left home. 'She came home very briefly once or twice after she'd left but I don't really count that,' said Thaw who saw his mother only once more, many years later in the early 1960s. She had died by 1990.

Yet he didn't regard himself as a deprived child. 'We had a lot of love from our father and from his family. In addition, there was a couple upstairs, Frank and Gladys Bell, who kept an eye on us when Dad was working. Gladys used to see us into bed and give us milk and biscuits for supper – very kind. I knew plenty of people whose families were "whole" who were far unhappier than I was.' Thaw also recalled with retrospective glee the occasions when he was allowed to go out with his father in the cab of the lorry – the big adventure of a trip to London, for example.

However, by 1990, the Mancunian lad who had left school at 16 and who used to speak with a broad north-west accent was accustomed to being consulted by his fans about classical music. Once Inspector Morse, lover of Mozart and Wagner, was an established television favourite, Thaw often received letters from viewers asking him to identify some of the background music. 'Sometimes there's a Beethoven quartet or something played, say, when they find the dead body and people want to know what it is.' Thaw told Lawley: 'I think that's marvellous because they wouldn't necessarily know about that music otherwise and go and ask for it in a shop, but they've discovered it through Morse.'

Perhaps this 'consultancy' role was bound up with Thaw's white-haired gravitas and sex appeal. Thaw, with likeable lack of vanity, laughed off the silver haired dignity first. 'Yes I do look older than I am and always have done from childhood. The hair is an inherited thing. My dad went white in his thirties too.'

His image as a sex symbol puzzled him more. 'I really do not know what this "thinking woman's crumpet" business means. They might as well be talking about someone else. I don't understand how it applies to me.' It was a source of much family mirth. Thaw said that his wife Sheila Hancock and their three daughters – all still living at home at the time of his *Desert Island Discs* programme – teased him uproariously about it. 'They like it best when I am washing up. "Look at that the sex symbol, " they say. Basically they just ridicule it.'

Thaw's second record, another highly emotional choice, was an aria from Puccini's opera Turandot. He first heard it, when, as a young actor, he was vacuum cleaning his Kensington flat. 'I was bowled over by the power of this singing which I could hear coming from the radio above the noise of the Hoover,' he said.

How did a working class, fruit market lad get to be a RADA student Lawley wanted to know, probably voicing the question for many of Thaw's admiring and curious public. 'I'd always wanted to be an actor and I suppose I had the gift of the goat [sic], but for someone of my background it seemed a very unlikely "posh" thing to do. Drama school wasn't for people like us. That was the prevailing attitude.' It was Thaw's father, still alive at the time of the broadcast and by then used to his elder son's fame, who encouraged him. He told him to give it a go if that was what he wanted to do. If it did not work out, he could always come back to Manchester and get work in the fruit market again, Thaw senior pointed out sensibly.

Of course it did work out. Wearing his only respectable clothes – a teddy boy outfit complete with drape jacket, 10-inch bottomed trousers and crepe soled shoes – he started at RADA in 1958. Two years later he emerged without a Manchester accent, which concerned his father and brother, but with both The Liverpool Playhouse and Vanburgh awards. The former was important because it guaranteed the young Thaw repertory work for a year. He was almost never without work for the rest of his career.

For his third and fourth records Thaw chose Elgar's Cello Concerto and, like almost all the most intellectual professional musicians and musicologists invited to be castaways, the adagio from Schubert's Quintet in C major, often described by the cognoscenti as 'the most perfect and beautiful piece ever written'. Like the earlier Sibelius and Puccini pieces, both of these are profoundly moving. 'Your choices are likely to make you weep as much as to bring you comfort,' observed Lawley dryly. 'Yes,' was Thaw's simple answer. 'More than likely. There are buckets of tears there waiting to be shed if I'm caught unawares.'

Some things are not said on *Desert Island Discs*. Presenter and castaway evidently have a clear understanding and agreement about what may and what may not be discussed. In Thaw's case, no mention at all was made of his first marriage although he and

Lawley talked at some length about Thaw's long and happy second marriage to actress Sheila Hancock. Unsurprisingly, the only record chosen that was not classical was one of his wife singing 'Little Girls' in the musical *Annie*.

There were also several mentions, amid affectionate laughter, of 'the girls' or 'our daughters,' to whom Thaw had often read Kenneth Grahame's *The Wind in the Willows* , his chosen desert island book. In fact, one daughter is from Thaw's first marriage, one from Sheila Hancock's first marriage, whom Thaw adopted, and one from the Thaw and Hancock marriage, so each girl is a half sister or stepsister to the other two. Thaw, however clearly regarded the three as his family without constraint or limitation and did not want any attention drawn to the fact that they were not full sisters. As far as he was concerned, the detail of their parentage had probably become irrelevant anyway.

He was, however, prepared to talk a little about a short separation between Hancock and him in 1988. She had been diagnosed as having breast cancer and had, he hinted, felt that, in a time of acute crisis, she was not perhaps getting the support and understanding she needed from a very busy and preoccupied husband. 'The only answer for her at that time was to get away on her own and sort it out, which is what she did,' said Thaw. He continued: 'She has had to accept that I have a job which requires more commitment than just going into the West End to do a three-hour show each night, but at the same time, I no longer work to the exclusion of everything else – least of all Sheila. And I've deliberately done nothing for the last five months since I finished the last series of Morse. But it was never a question of *if* we get back together again. It was always *when*.'

At about the same time, Thaw gave up drinking alcohol, dismissing his decision as something of a non-event: 'A bit like giving up sugar really.' Whether excessive drinking had had something to do with the temporary problem in his marriage was not discussed although possibly implied. It was another topic which Lawley had presumably agreed not to pursue too vigorously.

Thaw's first big television success, the one that made him famous, was *The Sweeney* in which he played the tough London policeman Jack Regan. Lawley asked him whether it had needed a lot of research. 'Well, I made a point of going to Scotland Yard and meeting a lot of policemen from the Flying

Squad. I made friends there, some of whom I still have.' He explained that overall the police liked the series and found it realistic. In addition, he emerged from the experience with tremendous sympathy and respect for the police, having realised just what a horrible job they do. 'I couldn't do that job – not in a million years' commented the peaceful, home-loving, Thaw – so very different from Jack Regan.

The Sweeney was always mentioned by critics in newspapers and by organisations such as the Listener and Viewers Association whenever uneasiness about burgeoning levels of violence on television was discussed. 'Yes it was violent,' admitted Thaw, 'and at the time, if we'd been making a series about traffic wardens, I'd have agreed that the violence was gratuitous. But we weren't. It was about the Flying Squad and it's the nature of their work that they meet a lot of violence on the job. And sometimes they have to use violence themselves in self defence.' This was a topic that Thaw had obviously been asked about so often that he had a well-honed response ready. He continued, 'There are certain programmes on TV which I think are a lot more violent than The Sweeney ever was because they glamorise it. And we never did that. The team behind The Sweeney had been docu-mentary makers, so they tended to shoot it in a very realistic way in order to show that much of what they were focusing on was not pleasant. People did get hurt and bruised and it mattered, whereas some of these American things seem to glamorise the fact that you can shoot down someone in the street or get a car and run a few people down and that's fine because they're only villains. We never had any of that stuff in The Sweeney.'

Different though Thaw the private man actually was from the tough, streetwise cop he played, his public often confused the two. Many were unsure just how much acting Thaw was doing to turn himself into Regan. 'Discretion is the better part of valour and they tended to leave me alone if they saw me in a pub or in the street,' Thaw commented with some amusement.

Morse was very different because he was quiet, more thoughtful and generally a more approachable character. So once Regan was a man of the past and Morse was in the public eye, Thaw found that more people were prepared to engage him in conversation, even though, at that time, Inspector Morse's given name had not been revealed. When Lawley asked Thaw about the mystery he told her that author Colin

Dexter had told him the name but that he, Thaw, was not permitted to divulge it. 'Morse is embarrassed by it and that's enough for me within the terms of the series' said Thaw, refusing to be drawn by Lawley's light-hearted probing. (The name was eventually revealed as Endeavour, several series later in the late 1990s)

Masonic Mysteries was a Morse story first broadcast in 1990. It was based on Mozart's *The Magic Flute*. The complicated plot was cryptically bound up with the freemasonry that underpins Mozart's masterpiece, and a lot of the opera's music was played in the course of the programme. It was while researching for *Masonic Mysteries* that Thaw went to see *The Magic Flute* for the first time and fell in love with it. It was not surprising, therefore, that he wanted part of its overture with him on his desert island.

After *The Sweeney*, but before Morse, Thaw starred in a television situation comedy – or 'sitcom' – called *Home to Roost*. This is seldom discussed now, having been largely eclipsed by his later work. He found it a pleasure to do and something of a relief after *The Sweeney*. 'People in the business think of me as a comedy actor, so there was nothing strange in my being asked to do it' said Thaw, especially as he thought television comedy the hardest thing any actor can ever do, and very definitely not a second-class activity in comparison with the purity of 'treading the boards' in a theatre. Thaw believed that some of Britain's best actors are its top television comedy exponents.

'TV comedy is an awful halfway house between theatre and TV because you have a studio audience in front of you. If you don't get a laugh from them, you think, "Oh my God, what have I done wrong?" Then you suddenly wake up to the fact that there is a camera beside you and you are in close-up so you think, "I'd better keep going." So for me, and I know for a lot of mates who do comedy, it's a very stressful situation – possibly the most stressful situation an actor can be in.'

So why did he go for television rather than theatre? Was it because theatre can give an actor a reputation but it is television that makes him or her a star? For Thaw, it seems to have been a question of choices and priorities. 'You have to decide whether you want to entertain as many people as possible or just 600 or so each night in Shaftesbury Avenue or elsewhere in London's West End,' he said, acknowledging that stardom brings it own problems. Thaw was essentially a private man who would have been quite happy without the 'attention' of stardom. 'But sadly – to me – it's part of the job,' he conceded. 'It's an occupational hazard of it all that you're not allowed just to entertain people for an hour or two. You have to be prepared to do other things.'

Yet, in 1990, the classically trained Thaw was still, like many actors, mildly regretting the big theatrical roles that he had not played. He wanted to play Lear and Iago. He even hinted to Lawley that there were plans afoot for him to play these roles in the early 1990s at The Royal Exchange Manchester. Sadly, as it turned out, nothing ever came of this.

Conversation returned repeatedly to Thaw's marriage, which was very clearly the most important thing in his life. At the time of his death in 2002, Thaw and Hancock had been married for 28 years. When he took part in *Desert Island Discs* their strong marriage was already 14 years old.

He joked about the quality of the soft furnishings in the matrimonial home. 'Sheila and I always had stiff necks and sore backs by Sunday evening after a day spent sitting over the Sunday papers. Then one day, we realised that we were probably sitting on the most uncomfortable chairs in London – so we bought six

lovely new ones,' he said, explaining why his chosen desert island luxury would be a very soft, very comfortable, armchair.

He laughed, too, about his imagined affair with Elisabeth Schwarzkopf, saying, 'Sheila and I always say that Schwarzkopf is the only woman in the world who could ever rival Sheila as far as I'm concerned'. He chose Schwarzkopf singing one of Richard Strauss's *Four Last Songs* as his seventh record, another intensely emotional and sophisticated choice.

Thaw was not a man to make life plans or to set himself goals. Instead, he leaned with the wind and went where it blew him. In 1990, it was wafting him towards yet another series of Morse. 'I think if I'm at all objective about it, then Morse is the best work I've done,' he said. 'It's a quality product. I act it well. We get good scripts and it's popular with the public, so with all that coming together I think it's the work which has given me the most pleasure.' He also believed that the character of Morse, beneath the gruffness, was a likeable sort of man – caring and gentle – whom the public actually came to admire.

John Thaw's final record choice was the searingly beautiful and poignant contralto aria 'Erbarme dich Mein Gott' from Bach's *St Matthew Passion*. 'It makes me cry,' he said, adding that if he could take only one record to his desert island, it would be this one.

There was nothing shallow, brash or aggressive about John Thaw, as this revealing interview made very clear. He was privately much further from some of the abrasive characters he immortalised than many of his admirers realised at the time.

John Thaw's *Desert Island Disc* Choices

Sibelius – *Fifth Symphony in E flat* Berlin Philharmonic Orchestra conducted by Herbert Von Karajan

Puccini – 'In Questa Regia' from *Turandot* , sung by Dame Eva Turner, London Philharmonic Orchestra conducted by Sir John Barbirolli (Covent Garden 1937)

Elgar – *Cello Concerto* (Opus 85) Jacqueline Du Pré, London Symphony Orchestra conducted by Sir John Barbirolli

Schubert – Adagio from *Quintet in C major* (Opus 163) Pablo Casals, Isaac Stern, Paul Tortelier, Alexander Schneider, Milton Katims

Charles Strouse and Martin Charnin – 'Little Girls' from *Annie*, sung by Sheila Hancock

Mozart – Overture to *The Magic Flute* Philharmonia Orchestra conducted by Otto Klemperer

Richard Strauss – *Four Last Songs* Elizabeth Schwarzkopf Berlin Radio Symphony Orchestra conducted by George Szell

* J. S. Bach – 'Erbarme Dich mein Gott' from *St Matthew Passion* Marga Hoffgen Stuttgart Radio Orchestra

(* John Thaw's single choice were he reduced to only one record)

Book – apart from the Bible and Shakespeare, *The Wind in the Willows* by Kenneth Grahame

One luxury – a comfortable armchair

No Re-Morse:
an exclusive interview
with Colin Dexter

by Victoria McKee

American-born journalist, Victoria McKee, has lived and worked in Britain since 1973. She has contributed over many years to *the Times, The Sunday Times, The New York Times, Harpers and Queens* and other quality publications in Britain and around the world. Robson Books published *Working it Out,* a book about workaholism and occupational health, in 1991, and she is co-author with Mary Spillane of *UltraAge,* a book about ageing healthily (Macmillan 1999). Pan published her *Be As Young As You Want To Be* in 2001. She holds an MA from The Shakespeare Institute at University of Birmingham and is a Fellow of the Royal Society of Arts. She has been interested in John Thaw since interviewing him in a caravan for a women's magazine on the set of *Inspector Morse* in the 1980s.

Colin Dexter is as 'unassuming' as he says John Thaw always was. 'John Thaw wasn't shy, just unassuming', he stresses. 'I think people maybe go slightly wrong about his qualities. I think "unassuming" is better than shy or private – though I've read those words many times in connection with him. It was as if all the time he was in a state of mild surprise that he should be the object of so many people's admiration all around the world'.

So, seemingly, is Dexter – whose literary dexterity lies behind the internationally successful series of *Inspector Morse* books and television programmes, which have so far been enjoyed around the world in 22 different languages. The TV version of *Inspector Morse* has enthusiasts from Australia to Zambia, with an estimated audience of over a billion. Morse videos have been despatched by helicopter to North Sea oil-rigs and bought by the US Department of Defense to show on closed circuit TV to US armed forces personnel.

John Thaw used to say of *Inspector Morse* 'I don't know what makes it so special. If I did I would be a very rich man'. Well, he was, by most people's standards. He was earning a reputed £1 million a year at the time of his death and enjoying beautiful homes in both England and France. If Dexter is also a very rich man, as he certainly should be, he chooses not to act the part. He lives in an unassuming house in North Oxford and drives an unassuming car. But, as Inspector Morse teaches, one shouldn't assume too much.

Though Thaw was daunted at being stopped in the street to have his photograph taken or his autograph demanded by Morse admirers, the author – who played a cameo role in each of the thirty-three two-hour episodes (even if some of his appearances 'got left on the cutting-room floor', as he puts it) – was usually content to let the actor have the limelight. Although occasionally it could rankle just a little that Thaw was more closely associated with Morse in the public eye than Morse's creator.

'We did book signings together', Dexter recalls with an impish grin, 'and I remember one woman had brought a book along and said to me, "I don't want YOU to sign it – just Mr. Thaw"'. He pauses for that to sink in. 'It's amazing, isn't it: I WROTE the bloody thing! But John was very gentle and kind about it', he recalls with good humour. 'But then he was always gentle and kind'. Whenever we filmed a scene with me in it he would joke, 'I am not the star today'.

Dexter modestly describes himself as 'a part-time scribbler', rather than as a world best-selling author. 'I spent all my life in education', explains the former grammar school teacher of Latin and Greek in Leicester and Loughborough who, as he grew increasingly deaf, went to work for the Examinations Board 'looking after languages' in Oxford. He retired from his 'day job' at the age of 58 in 1988, twelve years after the first of his thirteen Inspector Morse novels was published. Today, he still lives in a modest semi-detached house in North Oxford which looks more like the home of a retired schoolteacher than that of an internationally renowned writer. He drives an old, but not vintage, car. And it's a Citroën rather than a Jaguar.

The Dexter home is, coincidentally, close to the headquarters of the Thames Valley Police, to whom he is 'known', he admits – but in the nicest possible way.

Has he met any real-life Morse's on the Force? 'No', he laughs. 'And I hope there aren't any'. He likes to think his creation is unique. But one senior Scotland Yard detective, now retired, told me, 'I enjoy the books very much, as did many of my colleagues, and even if we don't know anyone exactly like Morse there are a lot of us who do complicated crosswords, like classical music and even have Oxbridge degrees –

though personally I don't do cryptic crosswords, just the *Daily Telegraph* short one. We're talking about people at the top, though, not the constables who make up ninety per cent of the Force. However, we wouldn't be allowed the luxury of working on just one case at a time, like Morse is'. He is less keen on the television series than the books. 'We certainly wouldn't be allowed to drive around in our own cars like that, for insurance reasons if nothing else', he points out.

'Morse is always six furlongs ahead of the field', Dexter notes, a phrase he likes to use in his books. 'But very often he's on the wrong racecourse'. However it usually just takes a small, often subliminal, nudge in the right direction from his faithful sidekick Sergeant Lewis (played also to perfection, Dexter feels, by Kevin Whately) to get Morse's hunches on the right track again.

Dexter feels that the casting of Thaw and Whately could not have been more perfect, even though, as Morse readers will know, Lewis began life as an older man in the books. Then, when Whately was so memorably cast in the role, Dexter subtly managed to make Morse's faithful sidekick grow younger in subsequent storylines.

Authors seldom have any say in the casting of a television series or films based on their works, so Dexter, although retained as a consultant on the series, was presented with a *fait accompli*, accomplished by a combination of Ted Childs, executive producer of the series, and Kenny McBain, its first director, who died tragically young of cancer. Childs, who had been producer of *The Sweeney*, was looking for a new vehicle for John Thaw when McBain, who had been reading Dexter's books, suggested Morse. Childs was apparently delighted that it was set in Carlton's Midlands TV region as well as with its potential for Thaw. It was also McBain who suggested Whately as Lewis, thus beginning a new partnership, destined, perhaps, to be even greater than that of Regan and Carter in television history.

But although the casting is something for which Dexter cannot take any credit, he is now unable to visualise anyone but John Thaw ever playing the role of Morse and says categorically that he 'will not allow it'. 'I wouldn't let anyone else play him – and I shan't', he vows. 'The copyright is mine and I won't allow anyone else in the role, even if Hollywood came to me to make a film of Morse'. He is quite emphatic about that. But after we discuss how many valid portrayals there were of other great fictional detectives, from Sherlock Holmes to Hercule Poirot, and even his favourite, Philip Marlowe, he adds, 'Well, at least I wouldn't the way I'm feeling at the minute', realising, perhaps, that it's never wise to say 'never'.

The television in Dexter's cosy little sitting-room is hardly used, he says. And, if it's switched on at all, it is by his wife Dorothy, a slim, gracious former physiotherapist who discreetly keeps out of our way during the interview. 'I'm not a television watcher and, in fact, hadn't seen John Thaw in anything at all before he started in *Inspector Morse* in 1986', he confesses. 'I'd not met him before, either, so we spent the whole first day just talking together, getting to know each other – and I guess I got to know him pretty well'.

He is proud to show a hand-written note to him from Sheila Hancock after her husband's death, saying 'John was so fond of you – and not just because you created his most successful character'. With it, she had enclosed a photograph of the two men together during filming at Christ Church, Oxford.

'Whatever has been said of John Thaw', says Dexter, 'He was never grumpy, always quiet and gentle – although he was a wonderful mimic and could really make you laugh, particularly with his Tommy

Cooper imitations. Only once during the entire filming process of *Inspector Morse* did I see him get fed up. That was when we went to Eton to film something one day because we couldn't get into an Oxford College – and then we couldn't do the scene because it was under the flight path to Heathrow. The scene was only about 25 seconds long but we couldn't do it in that noise. Well, John got justifiably cross and said that if we were going to film there someone should have checked it out first. That was the only time I ever saw him lose his temper. After all, you've got to be patient on the telly. You sit around for eight hours just to film eight minutes!' As Dexter is usually to be found as an 'extra' in a pub or party scene, he knows all about that.

Dexter's own marriage has lasted nearly half a century and produced two children, a son, Jeremy, who works in the bursar's office of an Oxford college and a daughter, Sally, who also works nearby at Oxford University Press. Thaw enjoyed a much-chronicled quarter of a century union with the actress Sheila Hancock. So why did Dexter never decide to marry off Morse? Or at least give him an attractive 'ex' who could keep popping into his life? 'Because it's always a mistake, like when my great hero Raymond Chandler got his Philip Marlowe married off in *Playback,* the last book he wrote. It was pretty dreadful! All the rest of the time the man was vulnerable and lonely and anxious and pessimistic with a bottle of Scotch. But as soon as you get married you daren't take a bottle of whisky home, or lust after a beautiful client'.

Yet the happily married John Thaw managed to exude that air of vulnerability and loneliness that helped to turn him into a reluctant sex symbol – a role he never liked to acknowledge. 'He could appear very vulnerable and melancholy which was just right for the character', Dexter agrees. 'But if Morse were married you'd have to have him spend half his time talking to the missus'.

Then we leave Dexter's house and head for the heart of the 'city of dreaming spires and aspiring dreams'. We jump on a bus to go to his 'local', a couple of stops further on in Summertown. Dorothy Dexter declines to come, but dutifully keeps lunch hot for her husband who seems to like to have his whisky in pubs, washed down by pints of hand-pumped best bitter, rather than at home – just like the unmarried Morse. But unlike Morse, Dexter positively insists on buying the first round, despite the fact that he could probably 'drink out' permanently on the offers of admirers who crowd around him as soon as he enters the pub. He is clearly well-known and loved here, but insists, 'I think one of the great crimes is to be reluctant to buy your round'.

Dexter is an enthusiastic imbiber of both beer and whisky – like Morse – although he knows it is as bad for his diabetes as it was for his diabetic detective. He clearly regrets the fact that 'John Thaw was practically teetotal – at least when I knew him'. There are 'Morse pub crawls' to some of the numerous Oxford pubs featured in the books, and one gets the feeling that it would be great fun to do one in the company of Colin Dexter. But Thaw made it a policy, at least during his Morse years, not to drink on the job – just as Sergeant Lewis, if not Inspector Morse, does in the books.

So Dexter and Thaw settled for a few sedate meals at The Randolph Hotel, where Thaw stayed during his Oxford sojourns, and chats over coffee in the caravan Thaw shared with Kevin Whately on the film locations. However, the actor actually celebrated finishing the final episode of the final series with a drink or two – and manfully downed pints when it was necessary for filming, once having to do so several times in swift succession. 'It was in the Randolph Hotel. Morse had

to drink a pint and then something was wrong in the shot so he had to do it again, and then someone noticed that the clock was showing the wrong time, so poor John had to drink a third pint fairly quickly – to the applause of the crew for his professionalism'. Thaw was different from Morse. He was no drinker and lacked interest in the kind of cryptic crosswords that fascinate both Dexter and the fictional Morse. Thaw's was a RADA rather than an Oxbridge education.

Thaw was also uncomfortable with the strong sexual interest Dexter has Morse so frequently exhibit in the books. In *The Dead of Jericho*, for example, the detective is going to visit a woman he fell for at a party and with whom he hopes to form a sexual relationship. Then he discovers she is dead. But Thaw went on the record to say, 'I didn't like the seedy side of Morse in the early books. He was a bit of a dirty old man. I didn't like that and I wouldn't play it. I hated the fact that he was sometimes rude to women and I told the writers I wanted that changed. I wanted him to be more sensitive'. He apparently felt he'd been enough of a womaniser as Jack Regan in *The Sweeney* and wanted Morse to be more cerebral than the previous 'Action Man' womanising role with which he had been associated for so long. If Dexter regrets any of that he is too full of admiration for John Thaw's talents and the special qualities he brought to the part to say so.

Dexter describes Thaw as 'extraordinarily intelligent and interesting to talk to – cerebrally Alpha'. High praise indeed, particularly in view Thaw's lack of the elite education from which both Dexter and Morse benefited.

The two men shared a love of classical music, however. Coincidentally, both chose the adaggio from Schubert's *Quintet in C Major* when they were guests on BBC Radio 4's *Desert Island Discs* programme.

'Thaw did not have the educational advantages that Morse and I had'. From repeated references in the Morse books to poorly written, ill-spelled and badly punctuated letters, reports, etc, it is clear how highly Dexter prioritises education. Although Dexter's father was a taxi-driver and his mother worked in a butcher's shop, having both left school at twelve, they encouraged Colin and his brother to work hard at school. Both gained places at Cambridge University.

Dexter attributes his love of classical music to his older brother, who also became a classics teacher, explaining, 'We used to share a bedroom and one night when he hadn't come up to bed I went downstairs to look for him and found him listening, with tears rolling down his cheeks, to the first movement of Beethoven's *Ninth Symphony*. He was fifteen or sixteen at the time. I was about thirteen and I remember thinking that if this music could move my big brother like that it must be something very special. Then I began to realise that there were experiences you could call aesthetic that I'd had bugger all experience of'.

It is ironic that this Cambridge graduate has arguably done more – except possibly for Morse himself – for what he calls the Oxford Renaissance than any of that university's own students: '[Morse] came to Oxford to read classics at St John's but didn't get a degree because he thought a girl he knew was more important. He went away, like Housman, without his degree', explains Dexter, a huge admirer of A E Housman, whose work provided the title for the book in which he killed off Morse, *A Remorseful Day*.

'There are now Morse societies and Morse tours of Oxford – all sorts of interest generated by Morse', says the 'part-time scribbler' who treasures an accolade from the Lord Mayor of Oxford for his knack of portraying both 'town and gown' with equal aplomb. He has a knack of combing real people and places with fictional ones in such a way as to make it difficult for all but those readers who are intimately familiar with the area to disentangle the two. Often he will use locally known nicknames for real places. 'So The Bird and Baby pub which I write about is actually The Eagle and Child near here. That's where Tolkien and C S Lewis used to drink every Tuesday', he volunteers.

John Thaw got to know Oxford pretty well during his years of filming there, 'although when he wasn't filming, he would spend most of his time in the caravan learning lines', Dexter says, 'partly because he got so well-known that people would stop him every time he went out. They always wanted to have their pictures taken with him. He would oblige even though he must understandably have felt, "For Christ's sake leave me alone."'

The geography of the city and its environs plays an important part in many of the stories, and its photogenic qualities have added to the success of the television series around the world. 'I'm always accurate about topography', insists the author, who often includes a 'map' in his books of the area in which the murder is supposed to have taken place. He also does this with the Jericho area of Oxford in *The Dead of Jericho* and of the Oxford Canal in *The Wench is Dead*. 'But the maps cannot be relied on for total accuracy in the real world', he reveals. 'I will change a street name or have an extra few numbers in the road. In the 'Jericho' book it was absolutely as Jericho is – except for the one street in which the murders took place (Canal Reach). Yet, when a house in that area was up for sale, the housing agent rang me up and blamed me because no one wanted to buy it because people had read that someone had hanged himself, and someone else been murdered, near there. So you've got to be careful'.

Mischievously, Dexter confesses that he makes up some of the quotes with which his work is liberally sprinkled, even those attributed to famous people like Aristophanes. 'You're OK with someone like Aristophanes because not many people are going to come back at you about that', he maintains. 'My Greek used to be pretty good, but not even I can read Aristophanes with any fluency. The quotes are a joke. Diogenes Small appears frequently, but if you look at his dates he died at six-and-a-half years old. No one ever notices'. Maybe now they will.

Morse fans also notice that certain landmarks have seemingly sprung up in the Oxford area *because* of his books. I asked Dexter how he could set Morse's first murder case, *Last Bus to Woodstock* (1975), in a pub called The Black Prince and actually feature the landlord of that well-known pub by name. Dexter chuckles. 'There *was* no Black Prince pub in Woodstock at that time', he points out, though there is a well-known one today. 'I was thinking of a pub called The Bear. But I discovered during one of my rare pieces of research that the actual Black Prince (1330–1376) was supposed to have been born very near Woodstock. (The Black Prince was the eldest son of King Edward lll, also called Edward and was given his nickname after the battle of Crecy at which his father wore black armour). A few years later, someone opened a pub there called 'The Black Prince'. I guess that is what you'd call "creative writing".'

Dexter began his creative writing in his mid-forties, so there's hope for any would-be novelist who is late getting started. He created Morse one day while on holiday in Wales, on a rainy day when he had nothing decent to read, rising to the challenge he set himself that he could write something better than the reading matter he had to hand (As a cryptic crossword addict, he clearly relishes challenges.). He named Morse, and his sidekick Lewis, after 'my two favourite competitors in crossword competitions: Sir Jeremy Morse, Fellow of All Souls, Chairman of Lloyds, a brilliant chess player and the brightest person I've ever met anywhere and Dorothy Taylor, a 92-year old woman who went in for crossword competitions as "Mrs. Lewis"'. It may not be coincidence that Dexter also served as a signalman in the army during his National Service doing 'high-speed Morse' as he puts it. But even if Morse's brilliant powers of deduction were inspired by those Dexter attributes to Sir Jeremy, the detective's characteristics mainly seem to mirror those of his creator.

Dexter, like Morse, is an atheist with a fondness for hymns –'and hers', he jokes – and the King James Bible. Like Morse, he has a hatred of litter: 'it hurts me more than almost anything else in life' and is an obsessive fan of BBC Radio 4's *The Archers.* 'I've been listening since 1953 and get invited to the parties though I haven't been invited to be on it – yet'.

Dexter also admits to a penchant for pornography. 'In another life I would have been a brilliant director of pornographic films', he mischievously maintains. Videos such as 'Topless in Torremolinos' or 'Copenhagen Red Hot Sex' keep cropping up in Morse's investigations and, indeed, Morse (in *Death is Now My*

Neighbour, 1996) chooses the latter as the one video he would watch if he knew the world was going to end in a week – and says he'd prefer the company of Kim Basinger to that of Mother Theresa, Margaret Thatcher or Diana, Princess of Wales.

Dexter also shares with his creation a red-blooded male appreciation of ample bosoms. They feature so regularly in his books that one female reader accused him of 'being a breast fetishist', he reports, looking not displeased. But he mainly goes in for another type of 'bird-watching' now and makes his character, Morse, also fascinated with ornithology. In the final Morse book, *The Remorseful Day*, published in 1999, he writes '... As men grew older (so Morse told himself) the delights of the natural world grew ever more important..'.

Like Morse, Dexter used to be frightened of flying and opted for trains whenever possible, though his frequent international tours to promote his Morse books have all but cured him of that. 'I once had to do fourteen American cities in seventeen days, sometimes flying twice a day, and I think that's the best way to cure pterophobia', he told me, freshly back from a flying visit to Germany where *Inspector Morse* has many followers. 'That's another new word in the books – like audial, a word I created to replace aural, and which will be in the next Oxford Dictionary'.

Like his character, the author carries a little more weight and a little less hair than he might like, but even in his early seventies, this impish little man (for he is considerably shorter than his creation) has considerable charm. I found him a delightful companion when he took me to sample the delights of 'The Dewdrop Inn'. 'I don't eat much but I do enjoy drinking', twinkled Dexter, ordering a double whisky and pint of best bitter for himself, and a pint for me. 'Have you memorised the last three digits of the serial number of that bill?' one man at the bar, obviously a Morse fan, ribbed him. Dexter is clearly well-known and well-liked at his local. Almost everyone nodded, waved or offered a seat to him. A clergyman engaged him in an earnest discussion of *The Proofs of Holy Writ* by Rudyard Kipling, one of Dexter's favourite writers.

Despite his severe loss of hearing he is as able to handle himself as well in conversational cut-and-thrust, just the title character in *The Silent World of Nicholas Quinn,* a Morse mystery dedicated to the profoundly deaf Sir Jack Ashley, then an MP, now Lord Ashley of Stoke. Dexter felt it translated successfully to television. But, back in the real world, at one point, he understandably mistook the clergyman's use of the word 'Restoration' for 'Resurrection', so the conversation took a curious turn. As the author noted in *The Jewel that Was Ours*, (1991) 'A deaf person ... is not so much worried about not knowing the answer to any question put to him; he's worried, embarrassingly so, about not hearing the question'.

That book is one of several 'based in part on an original storyline written by Colin Dexter for Central Televison's Inspector Morse series', as its blurb runs. Dexter explains, 'some of the stories were just plots for TV. At first I would write very detailed plots but later sometimes I'd just speak to the scriptwriters and say "why don't we have one episode taking place in Australia, about a supergrass", and give them only the very vaguest outlines'. He was pleased with the high calibre of the scriptwriters who included Anthony Minghella and Julian Mitchell.

'The only work I did in many stories at the end was just to go through the drafts. Often there were seven or eight drafts'. There were 'a few rows', he admits.'If you're writing a book you can let Morse have a telephone call that he can't have on television, because you'd either have to hear the other person, and then people would recognise the voice, or, if you don't hear it, Morse would have to say something about it to Lewis or somebody in order to explain it. So it's difficult to do'.

Much of the clever, cerebral sub-text of the books had perforce to be lost. When Morse enters a pub in a book, the author can reveal in fascinating detail what is running through his character's mind at that moment – from thoughts about the murder to appreciation of the physique of a woman sitting at the bar – whereas John Thaw had to try to convey all that in a look. He managed it surprisingly well. Dexter learned to live with the limitations of the new medium and doesn't appear to have had many temper tantrums.

Did John Thaw have any say in the scripts? 'Not heavily', says Dexter, 'but sometimes he would say, "this dialogue seems a bit wooden" and it would be changed – because he was usually right. John had a very good memory for dialogue, and was a very good master of dialect, so that he could convincingly play an aristocratic RAF officer in *Bomber Harris* or a South African in *Biko*. But he always said that Morse was the character most like him, and the one he most liked playing. He felt they were very similar'.

Almost, if not quite, as similar as Dexter and

Morse. 'Like Morse I have a lot of ideas – especially if I've been drinking a lot – but if I've been drinking a lot I tend to forget them', Dexter told me with a twinkle in his eye over his second double whisky at the pub. 'But I don't ever write in pubs – I've got better things to do there, like talk about who's going to win the two-thirty'. Yes, he shares Morse's penchant for the odd flutter on the horses – 'but nothing too serious', he stresses. 'I write sitting solitarily in my study, drinking a drop of Scotch. I write everything in longhand – twice – and then have it typed, because anything mechanical declares war on me'.

Dexter's 'interest in alcohol' is such that he ignores his doctor's advice to cut down his drinking in deference to his diabetes. Like Morse, he is a late-onset diabetic, dependent on four insulin injections a day. And, like Morse, he refuses to give up what, to him, is one of the great joys of life. 'I have given up most vices, but not alcohol – and I know more about the dangers of alcohol than most people', he says after letting his arm be twisted into having a second round. He would have been happier, in some ways, if John Thaw had shared this Morse-like quality but realises that it was probably best for the character that the actor was always so highly disciplined while working.

At least Dexter accompanies his drinks with peanuts, so that balances his diet a little. 'No, I don't eat them for the protein', he protests. 'I just like the taste of them with whisky'.

Morse, he notes, 'developed most of the medicinal conditions that I did – but a few years later. His 1989 adventure *The Wench is Dead*, winner of the Crime Writers' Association's coveted Gold Dagger Award, has Morse investigating an historical mystery while he is stuck in the John Radcliffe Infirmary suffering from a bleeding ulcer. Dexter had been similarly stricken several years before. *Death Is Now My Neighbour* (1996) deals with Morse discovering he has diabetes and reacting rather as Dexter did when he was diagnosed in 1985.

'Morse deserved to die a little before his time, the way he overdid the beer and whisky and because of his general lack of care for his health', says Dexter without sympathy. He claims he has no remorse for killing off his hero in *The Remorseful Day* (1999) irrevocably and, apparently, un-resurrectably (or restorably). But there are more personal reasons why Dexter is comfortable with that choice, although it seemed to many of Morse's millions of fans around the world an unnecessarily cruel and final decision. More cynical observers accused him of killing off the goose that laid the golden eggs.

But, as Dexter confesses with admirable candour, 'I'd lost all freshness anyway – or was beginning to. You can get a bit cliché-ridden if you're not careful. And I have no desire to create another character. I feel I've done enough writing. Although I was writing a television play called *Virgil: Honour His Ghost* for John Thaw, so John's death took the wind out of my sails on that. It is set in the 1960s and deals with the controversy of comprehensive versus grammar school education. John was meant to play a classics master at one of the traditional schools'. Dexter falls silent for a minute as he remembers how 'John knew I was writing it, even though he never saw it, and I didn't finish it until after he was diagnosed with oesophageal cancer in June 2001, I believe'.

But the main reason Colin Dexter does not regret comprehensively killing off Morse with a massive coronary is because he feels so strongly that he cannot visualise anyone but John Thaw in the role that the actor so memorably made his own.

Provence crosses the Atlantic

by Judith MacLean

Judith MacLean grew up in San Francisco Bay and attended Brigham Young University in Utah before completing a degree in nutrition at University of California, Berkeley. She and her husband, who is a special needs teacher, are great admirers of good British TV drama – such as series and one-off films featuring John Thaw – which they search out via satellite. She gives piano lessons and is a church organist, as well as breeding Maltese puppies and teaching classes in ceramics and doll-making. Judith MacLean has two grown-up sons, one of whom has just completed a masters degree in journalism.

When *A Year in Provence* was shown here in America, the general population knew John Thaw only as Inspector Morse. We first saw Morse here in 1988 on our Public Broadcasting System (PBS), which is non-commercial, and later on the Arts and Entertainment (A&E) cable network. It took only a few years for *Inspector Morse* to become very popular and to establish John Thaw as a favourite actor on nightly shows.

I remember when I first became aware of *A Year in Provence*. I saw a picture in a television guide of Peter and Annie Mayle (played by John Thaw and Lindsay Duncan) walking through an outdoor Mediterranean market. It was captioned *Spring in Provence*. So I was pleasantly surprised to see that Inspector Morse did more than just solve murder mysteries. Alas I had a bit of a problem. The spring episode of *A Year in Provence* was being carried on the A&E cable network and I did not subscribe to a cable system. Then came a flash of light. My mother was a subscriber. I telephoned her and arranged for her to tape it for me, knowing she would probably enjoy it as well. After the broadcast, she rang to tell me how much she had liked the programme, but that we had missed the first part, which had been shown a few months earlier.

What a wonderful treat it turned out to be when I was finally able to view the tape. Of course, I was anxious to see what I had missed in the first episode so I telephoned the network to find out about re-runs. The disappointing answer came was that it wasn't planning any. Tapes, however, were going to be made available. I jumped in with both feet and ordered a set – which I have never regretted because of the many pleasant hours my family and I have spent watching the series.

About a year later, I came across an interview John Thaw had given in which he discussed some of the other films he had made. I was immediately interested because I had always felt that an actor of his calibre must have made many films. I was delighted to discover that there were many series and single films. The problem was that most had been made for British audiences and were therefore difficult for me to access.

Then I read something that surprised me. When asked about *A Year in Provence*, Thaw had said, 'I had a disaster with that but we are all allowed one'. My first reaction was to re-read this in disbelief. How could he possibly consider it a disaster? My family and I, along with quite a few friends, who had shared my tapes or watched it on television, had all loved it. What he was saying simply did not make sense.

It made me curious so, with the help of my city library, I searched a newspaper database for some reviews of the series. I found fifteen of them, covering a wide geographical area here in the States. Only two were negative. The rest gave very positive reviews. This made Thaw's 'disaster' comment even more of a mystery. I felt at the time that the answer must lie in England. But life moves on so I left the mystery there.

I was distressed and very sad to hear of the premature death of John Thaw in February 2002. Shortly afterwards I was given the opportunity to write this piece about the Provence series. So now I had a reason to investigate the curious disparity in the reaction to *A Year in Provence* between the US and Britain.

As an American, I can only suggest, of course, what seems to me to be possible reasons for the adverse British reaction to the series. In Britain, *A Year in Provence* was shown in twelve weekly episodes. The first was broadcast on 28 February, 1993. The viewing audience started at 14.5 million, but by the final episode it had dropped to 4.7 million. I don't believe that this decline was on account of poor production quality. As a professional at *The Seattle Times* wrote 'A Year in Provence* is classy. This is not your usual fast-action TV fare, but rather an evenly paced, gently funny production with beautiful scenery and perfect casting. It should come as no surprise that the classy endeavour is a production of the BBC. With most of TV moving at a frantic pace and most TV humour broad and crude, this warm, gentle comedy is a welcome relief'.

I decided to try several lines of inquiry. The first was to find out what kind of publicity it had received. It was obvious that the BBC had very high expectations. *The Times* reported 'A Year in Provence* is the central plank of the BBC's £80 million assault on ITV this winter ... BBC 1 expects as many as 15 million to tune in'.

During the weeks *before* it was broadcast, the critics were giving it thumbs down, but their criticism was more against the book than it was the TV series. *The Times* reported: 'Peter Mayle has already ruined life in the Luberon and the television series will make matters worse. Mr Mayle, as portrayed by John Thaw, will doubtless make his smug progress through the seasons, ever-genial, ever-tolerant, ever-condescending towards those canny, oh-so-colourful French masons and their funny local mores. It will, I fear, be as fictional as *The Archers*, but less real and totally one-dimensional. In Mr Mayle's everyday story of French peasant folk, the only characters, save himself, are Joe and Eddie Grundy'.

Britain's *The Independent* wrote about it in the same vein, 'It was inevitable and, for a small band of middle-class francophiles, disastrous. Their corner of *la vieille Provence*, all pink-washed farmhouses and Elizabeth David, had been turned into a best-seller. But if Peter Mayle had blown their secret, the arrival of the BBC, Inspector Morse and a creative design team could ruin things for good. Do the locals mind? Not much, so far. They've survived Mayle, the book, but can they survive Mayle, the telly?'

In its lead-up to the start of the TV series, the *Daily Mail* ran a story about the previous owners of the farmhouse that the author, Peter Mayle, had purchased and subsequently featured in his book. It pointed out that the farmhouse was not quite the ruin that Mayle had made it out to be. This was also the case with the farmhouse that was chosen as the setting for the TV series. In fact, it had taken a great deal of money and the expertise of talented set designers to 'age' the building. In summary the article questioned how much realism has all this expensive fakery achieved? The TV series may be faithful to the spirit of Mayle's book. How faithful is the book to the truth? Mayle's account, he has said, is as honest as he could make it. Oh, really?'

Such cynicism was nothing compared to the criticism of Joe Joseph, of *The Times*, the day after the first episode was broadcast: 'Last night, BBC1 unveiled its much-vaunted twelve-part adaptation of Peter Mayle's *A Year in Provence,* starring John Thaw and Lindsay Duncan. Or did it? Had you missed the first few minutes, you might have been struggling to place the programme. Was Inspector Morse on an assignment in France? Had John Thaw landed a bit part in an episode of *'Allo 'Allo?* ... You can understand why Mayle, offered a fat cheque, agreed to sell the television rights, but why did a producer want to buy them? The book's bestseller appeal was that Mayle traded city life and office politics for a French idyll. But last night's programme would appeal rather less to armchair dreamers and rather more to fans of the *Carry On* films. Relaying the plotless drama by mixing dialogue and voice-overs looked less like a stylistic choice than a cop-out. Thaw and Duncan seemed rather classier actors than the script they had been given to deliver. Also, although it is hardly Thaw's fault, it was difficult to erase all recent memory of

Inspector Morse. You expected him to shout "Lewis!" at any moment'.

My second line of inquiry was into the scheduling of the programme in Britain. *A Year in Provence* was running against the established popularity of *The Darling Buds of May*. And, as if that wasn't enough, *Provence* began thirty minutes after *Darling Buds* had already begun.

So I think several factors contributed to *A Year in Provence's* disappointing reception. There was considerable spillover from the pounding Peter Mayle, the author, was getting for the influence, real or imagined, that his book was having on the French Luberon. Along with that, the BBC may have had over-optimistic expectations of a film that is as lightweight as *A Year in Provence*. When taken in short episodes, it really does not have the same level of dramatic impact that a popular sit-com would have.

John Thaw may have summed it up best himself during an interview he gave to *The Times* in 1994. 'It was only a harmless little half-hour series. It was just hyped up too much. It was successful in America. It was up for awards and they liked it in Japan', he says. 'But I think it came out of the wrong hole at the BBC. It was produced and directed by drama people. But we thought it was light entertainment. With hindsight, someone should have put up a sign at the start of every episode, saying "This is supposed to be amusing"'.

Yes, as he said 'It was successful in America'. Maryland's *Baltimore Sun* announced: 'A Year in Provence might be the most diverting and refreshing TV movie of the year'. The Phoenix newspaper, Arizona, described it as 'thoroughly delightful, lighter-than-soufflé'. And, in Pennsylvania, the *Pittsburgh Post-Gazette* set it up this way: 'We're here to endorse a kinder, gentler reality TV, one that's a world apart – literally – from cops on patrol and taken-from-the-headlines Sunday-night dramas. If you're going to indulge in escapism, why not escape to something pleasant – say, A&E's delightful *A Year in Provence*'.

Not only did we find it delightful here in the US, but evidently viewers in other countries found it charming as well. In London, the *Evening Standard* reported: 'The BBC television series of his (Peter Mayle's) book may have taken a nosedive in Britain, but it has become an outrageous hit in Japan. Since the £3 million series starring John Thaw and Lindsay Duncan was shown on Japanese television earlier this year, rural Provence has been invaded by "les nipons" as the French call them. The Japanese translations of *A Year in Provence* and *Toujours Provence* have both sold half a million copies'.

In an Australian paper, the *Courier-Mail*, a viewer wrote responding to the reprint of what was described as a demolition job by the television critic of Britain's *The Sunday Times*, Craig Brown, writing about the *A Year in Provence* series. She wrote: 'I loved it. I often find that my view and the critics' views differ, and this may just be one of those occasions. But I was so interested in the programme that I purchased the book the following morning. I found the characters realistic and not at all condescending or dull and certainly not blancmange-like (as Brown had suggested). I can't believe that I watched the same programme as Craig Brown'.

Almost ten years have passed since the television series of *A Year in Provence* was first released. The world we live in has changed and there is now an even greater need to slow down. What better way than to enjoy the atmosphere, the nuances and the pleasures of Peter Mayle's dramatised diary?

The casting of *A Year in Provence* was wonderful. The French actors were so skilled that many people I interviewed following a showing believed that the roles must have been taken by local residents. The diversity of their personalities is refreshing. You grow to understand and appreciate them more and more as the months go by, just as you would in normal life. Lindsay Duncan, as Annie, combines soft speech with strength. She is long-suffering but has her limits and will, when necessary, draw a line in the sand, which makes for visual, dramatic tension. The role of Annie Mayle was specifically created for the televised version because Peter Mayle's real-life wife, Jennie, is elusively understated in the books.

That brings me to John Thaw. If you have seen him only as Inspector Morse then it may take a few minutes to get used to the smiles and the happy way he walks as Peter Mayle. Then the thought may cross your mind 'isn't it nice to know that Morse has an alter ego that can enjoy a normal happy life'. In an interview with the Los Angeles *Daily News*, Peter Mayle, the author, explained that he was not entirely happy with the choice of John Thaw as the actor to play him. 'He was much too fierce-looking', said Mayle. 'I'm much more frivolous than that, much happier. I should think someone like John Cleese would have been a better choice'.

John Thaw saw it differently. He once said 'the

truth is, when I first took the job I knew I wasn't going to impersonate Peter Mayle. I couldn't do that because, although I'd met him a couple of times, I wouldn't know where to begin to impersonate him. I'd have to spend a lot of time watching him. So I thought I'd do it as a character near to me – John Thaw – but calling himself Peter Mayle. The first couple of days Peter came on set with his wife, I did feel a bit self-conscious. I was aware that here was the man whose name I had taken. It was a bit unnerving'.

The author, Peter Mayle also recalled being on the set. 'I would bump into them from time to time. I'd say to John Thaw, "How's it going John?" And he'd say, "Oh, it was a very tough week because we had the visitor who got sunstroke and diarrhoea". So I said, "What's going to happen next week?" He said, "I think the septic tank explodes". As I listened to this catalogue of domestic disaster, it was with a thrill of horror I remembered that it had been happening to me a few years before'.

John Thaw brought a quiet strength to the role, which gave the character authenticity. He carried you along with him and invited you to identify with him as he dealt with the pleasures and pains of settling into a new lifestyle in France. He also added depth to the role and was able to bring out the gentle humour which characterises Mayle's style. Thaw's silences are as articulate as his words.

The farmhouse that Peter Mayle wrote about in his books was not used in the television series. Tiresome tourists calling on him uninvited had already made Mayle's life difficult enough. An extensive search was made and a place was found that would work. It even had the necessary swimming pool. There was a problem, however, in that it had already been restored so it looked too good to be in need of the renovations Mayle described. So the outside of the house was reversibly aged with a layer of latex. Artists covered it with layers of pigment, which created the correct colouring for old stones. The shed and vegetable garden had to be added. The vegetables, the wisteria and even the grapes were plastic because the local farmers had picked their grapes a few days before the scheduled day for filming the harvesting episode. Five hundred bunches of plastic grapes had to be brought in. All the expense and work that went into re-creating the Mayles' home, and the landscaping around it, were well worth it, however. It was most convincing and evoked the alluring beauty that is the Luberon.

There were some animals in the cast, a very loud

cockerel, a number of goats, a rabbit, a pig and a dead fox. There were also two dogs that were prominent in the book but less so in the screen version. John Thaw explained: 'We had two Labradors, French born and raised. They were just, for want of a better word, useless. They would not do anything that was required of them. If you were in a scene and they had to walk towards you, they'd run round and walk the other way. I don't think they liked the English very much. There were a lot of scenes with those dogs scripted in the book, but you don't actually see very much of them. Maybe they knew something I didn't know'. You do occasionally see them running around the hills or sitting about looking noble, which they did particularly well while they watched Peter bury the dead fox their neighbour had kindly given the Mayles as a welcoming gift.

The series begins with a very spectacular lunch. And many interesting days begin with Annie either waking up slowly or rising up suddenly and calling out to Peter to get up because she hears, smells, or somehow senses that there is something going on down in their courtyard. The 'something going on' is usually their neighbour, who has arrived with an interesting gift or with a request.

When they lived in London, the Mayles would wake each day to the same old routine; now they wake up to a new adventure each day. The relationship between Peter and his wife Annie is realistic, refreshing, loving and respectful. They pull together and support each other as each of them takes a turn at being overwhelmed with the frustrations of their new life. The strength of their relationship adds integral continuity to the film. The force that moves the story along is simply the passing of time as you go from month to month. There should be no presumption of a plot because there is none. Life is simply being lived at a leisurely pace.

In the US, *A Year in Provence* was divided into four ninety-minute episodes. Each one was named after a season of the year. Winter: 'The initial episode was shown in March and was widely praised by viewers and critics' – *The Washington Post*, 9 May, 1993.

In the first part of the series you sense, with the Mayles, the feeling of being slightly unsettled. These are the problems that always arise when you move home. It's like buying a used car in that you never know what is going to break down next. The Mayles had visited the area in the summer but had not experienced any of the other seasons. When they wake up to the roar of the mistral (wind) and find their water pipes frozen, Annie asks, 'Is this normal?' Peter replies, 'I've no idea'. 'That's wonderful isn't it?' A confused Annie asks, 'What's wonderful?' Happily, Peter replies 'We don't know what's normal anymore'.

As they begin to address the problems they are having with their farmhouse, they begin to meet the men who will eventually transform their house into something more comfortable and develop friendships with them. This group of 'artisans' is led by their 'Napoleon', Monsieur Columbani, who turns out to be a very charming individual. The Mayles are also introduced to their very diverse set of neighbours. Amédée and his wife, Huguette, seem to live closest to the Mayles. They are also the caretakers of Peter's beloved vines. This stems from an old agreement that has long been in force. They do the work and get the largest share of the harvest, but Peter ends up with plenty of wine. Next is the mysterious Antoine Rivière. There is a Parisian aristocrat living nearby, Madame Eveline Hermonville. This woman is great fun to watch as she dashes through life in her own little world. Along the way she creates some amusing problems for the Mayles. We are also introduced to Marcel, the postman, who is not a neighbour but ever-present in the series. The Mayles seem to look to him for some of their early French language lessons.

The French language is handled very smoothly in the series. Annie appears to have a better grasp of it and she helps Peter and the rest of us by translating – not word for word, but just enough to give you a good idea of what is going on. When she is not around, Peter translates, frequently as a part of his thought process as he thinks aloud in English. A lot more French is spoken at the beginning of the series than at the end and this is very well handled. We have the sense of becoming acclimatised to the people and the language, just as the Mayles are.

When the series is divided into four parts, a mystery occurs in each one. In the winter part, the mystery involves truffles. There is a truffle godfather, a truffle agent, and there are duff truffles, Italian truffles and weighted truffles. There are also truffle-hunters in the form of flies, pigs and, of course, humans. Peter jumps headlong into the mystery and has quite an adventure because, of course, all truffle transactions are performed 'under-the-counter' to avoid the taxman, something Annie finds ironic as she used to be a tax inspector.

The *Wichita Eagle* said of the spring episode:

'Spring has finally sprung and it is time for a second delicious visit with British expatriates Peter and Annie Mayle'.

It also is ironic that the first overnight house-guest the Mayles have is a total stranger. He is a friend of a friend by the name of Tony. British actor, Alfred Molina, plays him. John Thaw discussed him and other members of the supporting cast in an interview with Russell Davies. 'But my job', Thaw sums up with a good-natured mock paranoia, 'is to stay here and try to stand up to this string of character-actors they're sending out to plague me. We've just had Jim Carter and Fred Molina here in quick succession, both of which are about seven feet tall. I thought "what is the BBC trying to do to me? Make me look like a dwarf?"' The interviewer comments, 'Thaw is not very big, but on, and around, the set he gives you the feeling that even if he were one of the relative unknowns in the cast, he would still command a certain quiet space'.

The mystery in the spring episode revolves around the Mayles' letterbox 'with an M on it'. The box and several other things disappear one day. Peter is not really concerned, but Annie and their neighbour are worried. It seems that Amédée has always considered Rivière and his family to be smalltime crooks. Things quickly spin out of control and Peter, with the help of Amédée, finds himself breaking and entering both the house of Rivière and that of his cousin Serge Coulon. It is not long before most of the Mayles' acquaintances are involved in some way and before it all ends Peter is accused of the attempted murder of a cockerel.

Spring closes with a look into the world of French bread. There is a baking contest and Peter and Annie have volunteered to write about it for a friend. Unfortunately, the baker they have chosen to write about has some marital problems and they must solve them before he will do any baking for them. In this story we are given a wider look at the village and at village life. I think the American audience finds the village aspect of the series very charming. The old villages of England and the rest of Europe fascinate us because we really don't have anything like them in our country.

The summer episode begins with a large number of guests all arriving at about the same time because the Mayles are not very efficient at keeping track of dates and invitations. As the workmen noisily install the central heating, the house is buzzing with enthusiasts still operating at the pace of life that Annie and Peter left behind in London. The Mayles slowly melt under the weight of their duties to their guests. It is a surprise that the person who has the answer to the Mayles' problem of how to regain their peace and quiet is the little grandma who doesn't speak (at least, not when her family might hear her). This segment always stands out in my mind as an example of one of the strengths of British films. Within minutes of being introduced to each of the seven guests we have an understanding of their personalities. Character development is a great strength of British productions.

The summer heat seems to awaken the 'type A' part of Peter's personality, the part of him he had tried to leave behind in London. He becomes involved in a *boules* competition. Peter and Annie lose miserably the first time they play. After all, Peter has had the audacity to challenge the number one player in town who also happens to be the truffle trader who may have sold Peter duff truffles earlier on. The same man is also responsible for giving the Mayles misleading information when they placed a bet on a goat race earlier in the day.

The defeat only makes Peter more determined to take some revenge, so he works even harder practising his technique. Finally with the help of an expatriate by the name of Parrot, and Mr. Columbani (apparently something of a *boules* genius), Peter arrives at the moment of sweet revenge. After some good coaching and a lot of practice Peter has improved to the point that he feels he will not only just win but that he can 'thrash' his opponent. He requests a rematch and manages to do much better. In fact he is at the point of a possible victory after a tied game when a sudden cloud burst postpones everything. This is actually a fortuitous interruption because it gives Mr. Parrot the opportunity to counsel Peter concerning what he really wants most as an outcome of the match. When Annie arrives later as everyone is celebrating the end of the game, Peter tells her he 'lost but he won'. He realised what he really wanted was not revenge but respect and he learned that to lose was to win the friendship of the men of the village.

The mystery in the summer segment is one Peter never solves – how to make fine wine. His vines are pregnant with grapes and it is crucial that he does the right thing with them. He puts his best effort into it, but in the end relies on Amédée and Huguette, who by now have become good friends. You come to respect Huguette for her many talents. She works very hard in the fields alongside her husband and even repairs their old lorry. One of the wonderful scenes that end this segment is when Peter, Annie, Huguette (who is driving) and Amédée are all jammed in the front cab of Amedee's big old truck which is brimful with the precious grapes. They start careering down a very steep hill on the way to the winery. The truck is obviously out of control so Peter leans over and says in an understated English way, 'What exactly did you say was wrong with the brakes, Huguette?' All's well that ends well as we see a jubilant Peter and Amédée celebrating a successful harvest by spraying wine out of an 'aluminium haggis'. This episode was nominated for an Academy Award in 1993 for best TV mini-series.

By autumn, although work on the Mayles' farmhouse is nothing like complete, they have become accepted as villagers. It is time to meet a few more of the local residents.

Madame Hermonville's friends finally arrive from Paris. She is ecstatic. Unfortunately, the Mayles' cockerel crows all night. Eveline is ready for war, and though they try hard, Annie and Peter cannot negotiate a peace. When one of her friends decides to take matters into his own hands and shoots the cockerel, Peter and Annie are forced to take sides. The result is rather sad, but through it all we are given a further glimpse into Madame Hermonville's 'dramatic' and passionate nature and she begins to seem more sympathetic. Then it transpires that Rivière and Coulon had deliberately set up the conflict because they wanted to irritate her into selling out at a low price so they could buy up her land. It works.

The final autumn episode features most of the Mayles' close friends. In an effort to contribute to village life, Annie has been helping at the village school by teaching the children English. Then there is an announcement that the school is to close. It needs repairs and has only nine students. It has been decided that in future the children will be transported to another village. The Mayles organise a campaign to save the village school. The local priest produces a plan that involves truffles. He wants everyone who can to donate one or more truffles, and with the proceeds they will buy the materials they need for a school. The men of the village will donate their time and repair the school building themselves. It seems a straightforward idea but there is resistance locally. The villagers are very sensitive about their truffle caches. No one wants to admit to them for tax reasons. When Peter and Annie discover that Rivière has the biggest cache, they try to persuade him to make a major contribution to encourage the rest. It turns out not to be quite that straightforward because Rivière is otherwise occupied in combatting truffle-poaching. What follows is a great little adventure that results in Rivière finally achieving a level of respect in the village. As a grand gesture, he comes forward and leads the rest in saving their village school.

Another problem is that 'Father Christmas' has just died and this has cast a pall of unrest over the whole village. None of the workmen are co-operating with each other. No work is being done on the Mayles' house and no one will give a reason. They just blame each other. They consult the village mayor after they are told that the problem is a political one. The mayor explains that there is a battle going on over who will be the new Father Christmas. It seems that each trade union, political party and every other faction in the village wants its own man to be the next Father Christmas. It takes Annie, who gathers the women together, not only to solve the village problem but also the Mayles' problem. The upshot is that Peter is asked to be Father Christmas. Since he is considered to be 'neutral' everyone agrees. John Thaw makes a splendid Father Christmas, which is about as far from his Morse role as you can get.

While they were living and working in London, Peter and Annie Mayle had spent many happy holidays in the south of France. The sunlit beauty, the food and the slower pace of life are what drew them there. They decided to go into semi-retirement with Peter writing books for a living in the place they considered paradise. Such an idea probably occurs to most of us at some time, but few of us actually do it. It requires courage, patience and dogged determination. It is one thing to fall in love with a place while on holiday there and it is quite another to make it your home. You have to deal with the everyday problems of life as the local residents do and, to really feel comfortable, you need to become a member of a whole new community.

A Year in Provence is a splendid story. It is full of rich characters, unforgettable atmosphere and an abundance of humour. John Thaw and Lindsay Duncan superbly capture the essence of being 'innocents abroad'. The small but important moments in life are acted out beautifully. John Thaw's acting skills could make any character he portrayed seem real. Think of the difference between Inspector Morse, sitting on his settee listening to Wagner whilst puzzling over an unsolved murder case, and Peter Mayle being pulled through the woods by a huge truffle-hunting sow. When she finds them, he pats her side saying, 'Good little piggy, good little piggy', and we see the fleshy rear end of the pig, who is wagging her curly little tail.

A Year in Provence stands up to repeat viewing. It is an antidote for the pressures of life. Although it didn't fare well in the UK, I urge John Thaw's compatriots to give it a second chance.

Thoughts of a Kavanagh QC fan

by Charlotte Davies

Charlotte Davies is a New Zealander. She lives in Auckland and has been a devoted fan of John Thaw's work for many years. She has a BSc from Massey University in Palmerston North and an MSc from Auckland. She is currently working towards a business degree. She has visited Britain – where almost all Thaws' work is set – several times as well as the United States and Australia. Her hobbies are reading, films and art, as well as scuba diving, swimming and home improvements.

Nothing as complex as the production of a television series, given how many people contribute to its overall quality – or lack of it – can ever be perfect, but sometimes it can be very fine. I found *Kavanagh QC* intelligent, absorbing and impressively well acted and, most importantly, it was enjoyable. What follows is my response to a few episodes that I consider outstanding.

When I sat down to watch the first episode of *Kavanagh QC*, John Thaw was indelibly associated with Inspector Morse in the minds of most of the people I knew. Even if they did not know who John Thaw was, they knew who Inspector Morse was. Some thought they were one and the same. So I was interested to see how this actor would go about shaking off the image of the grumpy policeman. He did not have the luxury of time and fading viewer memory that he had had between *The Sweeney* and *Inspector Morse*.

However, as the opening scenes of the first episode unfolded, it all appeared quite effortless. A new look with longer hair and an expensive suit, a few lines with a mild northern accent and all thoughts of Morse were gone. Of course, it was not the accent or the suit that made the James Kavanagh character take hold so quickly and convincingly, it was the talent and conviction of the actor playing him. True to form, John Thaw brought Kavanagh to life within the first few scenes. We were instantly presented with an intriguing new character to get to know and follow through his professional and private life.

Home life was one of the key differences between this new character and Morse. Kavanagh had a family and friends, problems to deal with outside of his work, including teenage children, and a recently troubled marriage. He was a highly regarded barrister in complete control in the courtroom, but far from in control and, at times, visibly insecure when dealing with his family.

The part of James Kavanagh was created specifically for John Thaw. Clearly, the producers had made a deliberate effort to establish the character as quickly and definitively as possible. In the first episode we are given all the basic facts about him through a plot in which he defends David Armstrong, a young man accused of rape, played by Ewan MacGregor.

Early in the story, we see Kavanagh in jeans and a sweatshirt sailing with his family. We learn of his working class origins and socialist political beliefs over a family meal, and see him defending his profession to his headstrong daughter after his uncompromising and clinical cross-examination of the woman accusing his client of rape.

In a clever touch, we are introduced to Kavanagh's wife, Lizzie. She is waiting for him at an airport, holding a card bearing his name in the way a taxi driver would. 'Mr Kavanagh?' she asks, 'Mrs Kavanagh?' he replies. We hear him ask his wife if she is bored with him – a reaction to comments made to him by her recently jilted lover – and learn that he has passed up the honour of being Head of Chambers in order to give more time to his marriage.

We first see most of the other regular characters in the series during a chambers' party on a boat, principally Jeremy Aldermarten, Peter Foxcott and Julia Piper. We are given a strong hint of what we are to think of Jeremy Aldermarten, when he points out with relish to Kavanagh and his wife that her former lover is at the party. He is dragged away by Julia Piper who tells him, 'You really are a total shit'. Julia's loyalties are also apparent when she tells Kavanagh that he should have taken the Head of Chambers position. 'You could drag River Court into the twentieth century,' she tells him.

It is noteworthy how these peripheral characters were developed substantially over the five series.

Peter Foxcott, in particular, in this first episode is uncertain about his new role as Head of Chambers and keen to make an impression. However, he is worried about being overshadowed by Kavanagh. 'I might have the title,' he tells Aldermarten, 'but it is still Kavanagh people look to for advice'. Actor Oliver Ford-Davies does so well with the character that in later series Foxcott has grown into someone regarded by Kavanagh as a close friend and adviser.

In an imaginative contrast to the inevitable wordiness of the courtroom scenes, several moments in the story are communicated wordlessly. This technique makes the medical examination of victim, Evelyn Kendall, especially powerful. There are also moments of light humour. Kavanagh is scolded like a schoolboy by a judge and told to stop fidgeting. Archetypal snob and bigot Jeremy Aldermarten believes he has scored a point over Kavanagh with the selection of a Cambridge graduate for pupillage rather than the 'red-brick' candidate he thought Kavanagh would support. Then he discovers that the Cambridge candidate is a young black woman.

When the case is over, we are shown the various advocates, both defence and prosecution, in friendly discussions over drinks in a local wine bar. It is refreshing to see these people portrayed as professionals simply doing their jobs, as opposed to displaying deep personal involvement, which is so often depicted by lawyers in television drama. Not long after the last episode of *Kavanagh QC,* was shown, a school friend of mine, a barrister herself, told me that despite not being much of a television watcher, she was going to miss seeing John Thaw's portrayal of an advocate. She liked his lack of the stereotypical histrionics and table thumping which pervade many legal dramas. He spoke as a barrister would, she said, rather than relying on the over-dramatised tirades favoured by so many actors.

In the final scenes of one episode, 'Nothing But the Truth', we witness Kavanagh's self-doubt and anger when he discovers that, despite his victory in court, his client is actually guilty. Kavanagh confronts Armstrong with this knowledge in his office. Kavanagh's anger and disgust and Armstrong's arrogance are shown through little more than the actors' body language. It is one of many such unspoken moments that add real punch to *Kavanagh QC.*

By the time the second series was screened, the style and mood of the show and the dynamics of the characters were well established. The stories were becoming even more complex.

'A Sense of Loss' is the fourth episode of the second series. Kavanagh and Julia Piper defend an 18 year-old man, Paul Warwick, played by Ruaidhri Conroy. Paul is accused of shooting and killing a female police officer during a burglary. Initially, he confesses to the crime in a police interview, but then later denies it. The episode has a very despondent atmosphere at the beginning, when we see Kavanagh and Julia discussing the case in a darkened room, listening to Paul's taped confession, interspersed with flashbacks of events on the night of the killing. When Kavanagh and Julia first interview Paul in prison they find him unhelpfully truculent. He ends up throwing his chair across the room. Despite this, or perhaps because of it, Kavanagh comes away believing Paul is innocent.

The trial takes place in a small industrial town with a skyline of gloomy chimneys, adding to the mood of depression and futility. Paul lives with his mother and brother, who is brain-damaged from a car accident in which Paul was the driver. In a private conversation with Kavanagh, a local constable, PC Waller, describes his bosses' previous lack of interest in the housing estate he has been watching go downhill for years. He is cynical about the motives behind their current concern. He wishes Kavanagh luck. It is clear that Waller, too, believes Paul is innocent.

We learn that the dead police constable, Clare Kemble, 'went the extra mile' with her work by putting in time at a local youth club frequented by Paul. She was one of the few people who believed that he was capable of leaving his troubled youth behind him and going straight.

As more information is gathered, Kavanagh comes to the conclusion that Paul is protecting his brother, but cannot use this as a defence without Paul's permission. He continues to stay silent, and frustration begins to build. The only defence left is to 'sling mud' at the prosecution case. Anna Chancellor, as Julia Piper, has a pleasing moment during her cross-examination of a police detective when she unintentionally implies that evidence was planted. As a result, Paul's criminal record can be presented to the jury. The look on her face when she realises what she has done, and her consequent grovelling to the judge is skilfully acted.

When Kavanagh recognises that he has to put Paul in the witness box to have any chance of winning, Julia doubts the wisdom of his decision, saying that the prosecution, Peter Foxcott, will 'wipe the floor with him'. But that is what Kavanagh wants because he hopes that his client might finally tell the truth. 'Good,' he replies, 'unless he gets hurt he is got no chance of helping himself'. Both of them are right, as things turn out. Oliver Ford-Davies is masterly as QC Peter Foxcott, polite and charming with one question, ruthless and penetrating with the next. Having used Foxcott to rattle Paul, Kavanagh then upsets him further until he finally breaks down and admits that he is protecting his brother.

The scenes between John Thaw and Ruaidhri Conroy, both at the prison interview and the confrontation in court, vibrate with dramatic tension. Kavanagh becomes visibly frustrated with Paul in court and is clearly on the verge of losing his temper with him, while Paul struggles to carry the responsibility for keeping his family together by taking the blame for his brother's actions. The pressure, fear and anger finally defeat him under a barrage of questions, and we see Kavanagh relax as he senses that Paul is finally going to defend himself. When Kavanagh sits down after Paul's testimony is over, there is no smile, sense of victory or even relief. Thaw just evinces a world weariness.

Emotions run high again as the police drag Paul's

brother screaming from the court, with Paul and his mother fighting to free him. The mother turns on Paul, telling him that it is his entire fault, and then on Kavanagh. 'They'll never let me have him back again, thanks to you,' she tells him.

It is a clever piece of writing presented through some raw and harrowing acting. It was gripping television. A recurring theme in many episodes of *Kavanagh QC* is the tension between law and justice. The gruelling nature of this story is a powerful comment on real-life 'no-win' situations. Kavanagh sums it up in the final scene. 'I've known sweeter victories,' he tells Peter Foxcott. 'I think we'll mark this one down as a no-score draw.'

The sixth and final episode of the third series, 'In God We Trust', sends Kavanagh to Florida to help Julia Piper represent a man on Death Row. The character of Julia Piper left the programme at the end of the second series, but the chemistry between Anne Chancellor and John Thaw returns immediately.

The main plot of this episode focuses on William Dupris who has been convicted of murdering a family of four when they disturbed him as he burgled their home. It is a complicated plot involving political cover-up, drugs and racism and some of the peripheral char-acters seem a little stereotyped at times, but it is the smaller sub-plots that make this episode interesting.

When Kavanagh and Julia are held up at gunpoint in a car park, a moment of genuine fear is defused with unexpected humour by the look on Kavanagh's face when Julia pulls her own gun from her bag and scares away the would-be mugger. 'Drop your gun. Give my friend back his wallet, and get lost,' she says, dead pan, 'There's a good chap.' The look of utter disbelief on John Thaw's face during this exchange is remarkable. The camera is on him as the stunned mugger mumbles 'Shit', the exact thought in Kavanagh's head as he stares at the gun in Julia's hand. The shock of it all sends the conveniently pregnant Julia into premature labour and so, of course, Kavanagh has to take over the case. This device leads to some good scenes for Anna Chancellor, who manages to be suitably distraught without descending into the realms of melodrama.

Another memorable moment is when Kavanagh's case completely falls apart in court. One by one, his witnesses are discredited by the prosecution, which contrasts with what usually happens to Kavanagh in court. 'I walked into that court with a pretty good case,' he tells his client, 'and in less than three hours the prosecution demolished it'. When Kavanagh admonishes Dupris for not telling him everything he knew about the witnesses, Dupris replies with an insight that is perhaps as much directed at the audience as at his advocate. 'You isn't here for me man, you here for you. So don't go tryin' to tell me different. You here so when you go back home, all your rich white liberal friends gonna pat you on the back and say, "That Kavanagh, he is so fine for tryin' to help those poor dumb niggers."'

Lisa Harrow, who played Kavanagh's wife, Lizzie, had asked to be written out of the series. So while Kavanagh is in America, his wife is seriously ill at home and keeping it to herself while she goes through a series of medical tests. This adds poignancy to Kavanagh's telephone calls home. Both actors convey a great deal of 'between-the-lines' emotion. When Kavanagh asks Lizzie if she is okay, she tells him that she is just tired. It is a touching moment of dramatic irony for the audience, who knows the truth.

Kavanagh fails to free Dupris, who is executed. He does, however, expose the politicians behind the cover-up and returns home to Lizzie tired and jaded. The underplayed realism comes through again in the final scenes on Kavanagh's boat, when Lizzie finally tells him she has terminal cancer. No sooner has she revealed that she is dying than she is talking about having to get everything organised and planned. She loses her temper with him while he struggles to take in the news. It is unreasonable behaviour, but both human and realistic.

In cinematic style, the first ten minutes of the first episode of the fourth series, 'Momento Mori', starts telling us its story with nothing more than a little incidental dialogue. We see Dr Felix Crawley, played by Tom Courtenay (John Thaw's old friend, RADA contemporary and one-time flatmate), giving his wife a cup of tea in bed and heading off to start his day. Cut into this are scenes of Lizzie Kavanagh's funeral. Other than the singing of the congregation, the entire funeral is shown without a word spoken. Dr Crawley's wife packs a suitcase and, as she is about to leave the house, collapses on the stairs unable to breathe.

These scenes establish the two principal story lines of the episode. The main story is Kavanagh's defence of Dr Crawley, who is accused of murdering his wife by poisoning her with lithium. The secondary story is about Kavanagh coming to terms with Lizzie's death. He moves into a new house with the help of his children and tells them that he is in no hurry to get back to work. Soon afterwards, he finds himself watching a quiz show on daytime television and decides that it is time to resume office life. He comes home from a night out to find his daughter Kate sitting on the stairs in tears. The next morning they talk about their loss over breakfast. When Dr Crawley asks how he copes with being a widower, Kavanagh replies 'I take each day as it comes'. John Thaw injects quiet sadness into Kavanagh's whole demeanour. It is a subtle melancholy, interspersed with moments of humour, which Thaw conveys with a light touch.

When boredom finally drives Kavanagh back to work, he picks through the list of cases available with chambers' clerk Tom Buckley and is tempted by the Crawley murder case, especially when he discovers that Jeremy Aldermarten is prosecuting. 'Why didn't you say so straight off?' he berates Tom when he finds out. 'Well sir, I didn't want you to think I was spoiling you, first day back and all.'

Another new junior, Emma Taylor, is introduced in this episode. Emma, however, is refreshingly different from the succession of juniors who came and went after the departure of Julia Piper at the end of the second series. Kavanagh walks into his office to find that Emma has taken it over while he is been away.

She is clearly not intimidated by her surroundings or by the more senior members of chambers. She quickly puts Kavanagh to work helping her pack up her things. She refers to Jeremy Aldermarten as Jerry and is under no illusions as to the motives behind his generosity in offering to share his room with her when she has to vacate Kavanagh's office. 'He'll be hoping to get his leg over I expect,' she tells Kavanagh, leaving him speechless. Her direct, no-nonsense manner means that she and Kavanagh quickly form a friendship, despite being on opposite sides of the murder case. Emma is Aldermarten's junior, while Kavanagh is paired with the slightly ludicrous Rowena Featherstonehaugh, 'pronounced Fanshawe'.

As the case begins, we learn that, 30 years earlier, Dr Crawley had been accused of 'impropriety of a sexual nature' but was cleared of all charges. As he discusses this with Kavanagh outside the courtroom, we are given a first glimpse of his true nature by the odd expression on his face when Rowena casually removes a stray hair from Kavanagh's shoulder. It is a small thing, but evidently he infers a great deal from it and brings it up in discussions with Kavanagh days later during a consultation.

Tom Courtenay is excellent as the doctor, who

initially appears reasonably normal, but whose true character is gradually revealed and who eventually turns out to be a serial killer. His public image is one of a polite, humble man dedicated to his patients. The mother of a young woman named Alison Lucas, who died in his care, goes to court to offer her support and tells Kavanagh that the doctor is 'nothing but good'. She later discovers otherwise. As she sings his praises, Crawley remains impassive.

During a consultation with Kavanagh, Crawley condemns the immorality of modern society and young women who throw themselves at the likes of him and Kavanagh. 'Like that girl of yours,' he says, referring to Rowena. 'Once they get their claws in, decent sensible chaps are led astray ...' During Crawley's tirade, in which he claims that these young women unleash 'all the evils in the world', Kavanagh becomes increasingly uncomfortable.

Under cross-examination Crawley loses his temper and lets his arrogance show. 'I'm a doctor Mr Aldermarten. If I'd poisoned Anne, you wouldn't know about it, believe me. The means of bringing about a death by natural causes are at my hands daily ...' he yells. Tom Courtenay's acting here is excellent, finding the cracks in his character's facade and then just as

quickly covering them up again as Crawley regains his composure.

While awaiting the jury's verdict, Kavanagh and Crawley talk again. The doctor tells Kavanagh once more that he did not kill his wife. Then Kavanagh borrows Crawley's pen to sign some documents. The inscription on it indicates that it had been a twenty-first birthday gift from her parents to Alison Lucas, Crawley's patient who had died of a 'drug overdose.' Crawley claims that the pen was a gift from Alison's parents, but Kavanagh's suspicions are aroused and he uses his courtroom skills to play on Crawley's arrogance. Crawley states that if he had poisoned his wife, he would not have used anything as obvious as lithium. The matter-of-fact way Crawley talks about how to poison people and never get caught is chilling. He goes on to say that, for young people, he would use something that would pass as an overdose of street drugs. Kavanagh later learns from Alison's mother that the pen was not given to Crawley. It disappeared after her death.

The doctor is found guilty of killing his wife. Kavanagh confronts him with his suspicions. Crawley still claims that he did not murder her, but admits to poisoning Alison Lucas and counts off another five victims on his fingers as casually as if he were remembering items on a shopping list. When Kavanagh asks him why, he replies, 'I had my reputation to think of after that bitch when I was junior houseman. They ruin you ... pretend they're available, lead you on, and then "Rape!" I couldn't let that happen again.'

It is a treat to see two top actors like Tom Courtenay and John Thaw working together. The scenes played by the two of them alone in a darkened room, as the demented nature of Dr Crawley's mind emerges, are electric.

The second episode of the fifth series tells the story of two young people, Michael Woodley and Annie Fisk, who have run away from home together and arrived in London. They are alone and unfamiliar with the city, but clearly in love and hopeful about making a new start together. Michael promises Annie he will always look after her and never let anyone hurt her again.

We next see the same couple three years later. They are struggling to live in a run-down flat with a gas leak. Michael, we find out later, has recently got himself off heroin and is trying to help Annie to do the same. He goes home and they quarrel when he finds out that she is back on drugs. So he storms out of the flat, stops to light a cigarette to calm himself down, then returns to the flat, but he has locked himself out. He watches Annie through he letterbox flap in the front door and calls out to her. Then, seconds later, the flat explodes. Michael blames himself and tells a neighbour's nurse and a police officer that he killed Annie. It also turns out that Michael has a previous conviction for arson.

He refuses to help himself and sits in silence as his solicitor and Kavanagh try to get him to tell them his version of what happened. One of the few things he will talk about is his love for Annie. His describes his efforts to help her overcome her addiction, by quoting W. H. Auden:

If equal affection cannot be,
Let the more loving one be me.

Unhappy with the official autopsy report on Annie, Michael's solicitor arranges for a second autopsy. Annie, it is discovered, was pregnant. When Kavanagh decides to withhold this information from Michael, it presents an interesting moral dilemma, which is highlighted so frequently by the junior on the case, Martha Miller, that it starts to become as irritating for the audience as it is for Kavanagh. His decision is based largely on his personal feelings about Michael. 'He is 20 years old,' he tells Martha, who accuses him of playing God. 'If we get him off this, I want him to have a life afterwards.'

Kavanagh's silence about the pregnancy also prevents him from being able to reveal in court the incompetence of the doctor who performed the original autopsy. Nevertheless, he does have a quiet word out of court after the doctor's testimony is over. 'You're bloody lucky I didn't rip you to pieces in there,' he tells the doctor in a quiet, but menacing tone, 'because believe me, it would have given me a great deal of pleasure'. This secret is, in the end, what finally pushes Michael to tell his story when Kavanagh bends the rules by telling Michael in court about the pregnancy.

When Michael's parents visit him in prison, it is apparent that his relationship with them, especially with his father, is distant and strained. He storms out of their brief meeting because he can't get his father to look at him.

The parents are in court every day and although Michael's mother would clearly like to see him, his father refuses for both of them. They won't see their son even when Kavanagh offers to arrange it for them – much to Kavanagh's consternation. 'I've got a son. He is about the same age as Michael. And there are times when we keep our distance. I know how it can be,' Kavanagh tells Mr Woodley, and urges him to speak to Michael in case the verdict goes the wrong way and Michael has to face a life sentence. Mr Woodley tells him that he doesn't understand the situation between himself and his son. 'You're his father. He's your son. Full stop. That's all there is to it,' Kavanagh replies.

'You say you loved her. You say you did not kill her. Why aren't you helping yourself, Michael? I don't understand it,' Kavanagh asks Michael before they head into court. 'You sound like my father,' Michael replies. The episode makes several references to the relationships between fathers and their children. Kavanagh and Eleanor Harker discuss their own youthful relationships with their respective fathers.

Michael clearly affects Kavanagh on more than a strictly professional level. While on a weekend trip to the countryside with Eleanor Harker, Kavanagh surprises her by referring to his client as Michael. 'I don't often hear you call your clients by their first names,' she comments. Kavanagh is, to some small extent, taking on the role of Michael's surrogate father. 'When he smokes – Michael – I can't take it seriously, I have to stop myself from telling him off,' Kavanagh tells Harker.

Hugh Dancy plays the role of Michael superbly, creating a strong affinity with both the audience and John Thaw. During their final meeting before the trial ends, Kavanagh tries one last time to get Michael to communicate with him and agree to go into the witness box. 'I have never before gone this far with so few instructions from any client, which makes you pretty unique,' he tells him. 'But here's the real truth, Michael. Unique or not, I'll forget about you. You'll blur in the memory. But you won't ever forget the mistake you are making.'

Although he remains silent, we can see in Michael's eyes that Kavanagh may have finally got through to him. As everyone returns to the courtroom, Michael finally agrees to testify. He is initially hesitant, but under Kavanagh's questioning, eventually admits that he took the blame for burning down a doctor's surgery in his home town to protect Annie. She had been forced by the doctor and her parents to have an abortion and the arson was her revenge. Following this, they ran away to London. At this point Kavanagh realises that he can no longer keep the secret of Annie's second pregnancy from Michael. He quotes Auden back to Michael and adds, 'Annie was pregnant again, when she died'.

Kavanagh is reprimanded for his actions, and we are left to decide for ourselves whether he told Michael as a professional strategy or for more personal reasons. Michael's distress at hearing of the pregnancy leads him to explain what really happened to Annie and what he meant when he said he had killed her. He tells the court that when he looked through the door flap, he had seen Annie standing by the fireplace where the gas leak was, but he could not see her face. Then she took out a book of matches and turned to look at him. 'She looked at me, Mr Kavanagh. She was saying sorry. She was looking at me.' He explains that she would never have done it if she had known she was pregnant, but 'she shook her head a little and lit a match'.

'I killed her, you see. I didn't save her. No one saved her. None of us. Do you see?' Hugh Dancy's performance is outstanding throughout the episode, but particularly so in this speech. The scenes between him and John Thaw bring a real sense of humanity to both their characters. It lifts this story above the others in the series.

Michael is found not guilty. When we last see him outside the court, he is with his parents. We are left to infer that reconciliation is possible now that the truth is out.

The final episode of the final series has Kavanagh returning to a case from 13 years earlier when he represents James Cracken in an appeal against his conviction for armed robbery and murder. It is an episode in which Kavanagh is under pressure from a number of sources and it provides John Thaw with the opportunity to show Kavanagh's professional and personal vulnerability. Peter Foxcott is retiring and wants Kavanagh to take over as Head of Chambers. Eleanor Harker is considering taking a job in The Hague, and Kavanagh is feeling guilty over his performance in defending his client in the initial trial 13 years earlier. Before that trial was over, he knew for certain that his client was innocent, having met the real culprit. As a result of all these influences, Kavanagh is grumpy and miserable through much of the episode.

In 1985, three men, armed with shotguns, robbed a petrol station and, in the process, a school teacher and one of her students were killed. One of the three men arrested, James Cracken, was represented by Kavanagh and a QC named Sir Ronald Tibbit as senior defence counsel. One of the other defendants, Kevin Fowler, who is Cracken's cousin, named Cracken as a co-offender. Cracken claims that this is because Fowler found out Cracken was having an affair with Fowler's wife.

Although Kavanagh questioned some of the tactics Tibbit used in Cracken's defence, he did not say anything to anyone else, which he came to regret when Cracken was convicted. By the time of Cracken's appeal, Tibbit is dead and Kavanagh's sense of guilt over his inaction has been stewing for 13 years. The stress starts to show when, uncharacteristically, he snaps at his junior Martha Miller when she questions him. 'I know what I should have done Martha, but I didn't. I'm not exactly proud of it.'

To add to Kavanagh's worries, Peter Foxcott informs him that he is intending to retire for health reasons and wants Kavanagh to take over as Head of Chambers. It is a job Kavanagh does not particularly want, as he explains to Eleanor Harker. 'Nothing I want less. I'm not sure I could do the job, apart from anything else.' But he does not want to disappoint Foxcott. 'I owe that man a lot. I just never thought I'd be put on the spot so soon.'

Then, to make matters even worse, Eleanor Harker tells him she is considering taking a job prosecuting war criminals in The Hague. He even grows jealous when he first sees Eleanor with the young man who is recruiting her for the job, Filipe Arrabal. Eleanor introduces him to Kavanagh and Martha, then quickly leaves without further explanation. When Martha comments on how attractive Filipe is, Kavanagh goes into a quasi-Morse-like sulk. It is a funny moment amid all the seriousness, which Thaw plays to perfection. Seeing these chinks in Kavanagh's armour adds greatly to the series and it is a shame we were not shown more of them.

While in consultation with Cracken, Kavanagh learns that during the first trial, Sir Ronald Tibbit had visited Cracken alone and persuaded him not to testify on his own behalf. As part of the appeal, Kavanagh has to criticise the performance of Tibbet in Cracken's original trial. This makes him very unpopular with the judges in the case, as Tibbet had gone on to become a judge. It also raises again the question of why Kavanagh did not say anything at the original trial.

The anti-establishment tone that permeated the series from the beginning is emphasised in this episode. Although Cracken was originally sentenced to life imprisonment with a recommended minimum of 15 years, and has served 13 of them, he is now condemned to the full life sentence because he once protested his innocence from the roof of the prison. His solicitor comments to Kavanagh 'It's a double bind. Shout your innocence from the rooftops and you kiss goodbye to the chance of parole. But admit your guilt, even if you didn't do it, and it is much rejoicing as a sinner repenteth. Pre-release rehab classes and out you go.'

When Cracken's appeal is denied, while the other man convicted alongside him goes free on a technicality, he starts hurling abuse at the judges for playing word games with his life and is dragged from the court in tears. All Kavanagh can do is tell him how sorry he is, which does not mean much to Cracken. 'Just piss off,' he says as he is taken away.

Over a beer, Kavanagh commiserates with the solicitor's clerk. 'Why can't we put things right when we've got them wrong?' he asks, fuming. The clerk gives him a last word of advice. 'Don't let the bastards grind you down.' This spurs Kavanagh into accepting the position of Head of Chambers, perhaps in the hope of asserting more influence in fighting 'the establishment.' The episode ends with Kavanagh and Foxcott fishing at Foxcott's country home, finding comfort in each other's friendship. It was the end of the series, although there was still a one-off episode to come.

'The End of Law' is about murder, politics and industrial espionage. Wealthy businessman Alan Rainer returns to his hotel room to find a young woman searching his belongings. He kills her, unaware that he is being watched on a hidden video camera. When he runs from the hotel, one of the men who witnessed the murder and recorded it on video stops him on the street and, after a brief argument, convinces him to return to the hotel. We then see Harry Hatton, who had been staying in the adjacent room, standing trial for the murder after the body was found in his room.

Solicitor Advocate Sarah Swithen is left to defend Hatton on her own after the senior defence counsel is dismissed by Hatton for advising him to plead guilty and take a lesser sentence. Hatton is found guilty and his daughter, Alison, hires a private investigator while Sarah prepares an appeal. When she can find no obvious grounds for one, she turns to Kavanagh for help, but he cannot find anything either and advises her not to pursue the appeal.

In the meantime, Lord Cranston, a friend from the past, has approached Kavanagh to ask if he would consider becoming a judge. Kavanagh is already a Recorder and, as Peter Foxcott puts it, those in the courtroom eat out of his hand. A young barrister defending a woman accused of shoplifting strikes a chord with the idealist in Kavanagh when he quotes to the jury, 'The end of law is to preserve and enlarge freedom'. These scenes are a chance for John Thaw to turn on Kavanagh's charm and offer an intriguing glimpse into other sides of his character.

Kavanagh discusses the prospect of becoming a judge with Peter Foxcott, who tries to talk him out of it. Kavanagh explains his reasons for considering the new role. 'What about having a view of the whole picture? Not just those little bits of it we want the jury to see, that we persuade them to concentrate on in the interests of our client. But the whole picture. Having a view, expressing it. Seeing where justice lies.'

The offer clearly means a lot to him, which allows us to share his frustration when he is asked to compromise his professional integrity in order to take that opportunity. John Thaw lets us see that frustration simmering and building throughout the episode until Kavanagh's disappointment and disillusionment come to a head in the final scene.

Before things have progressed very far with the Hattan appeal, Kavanagh is advised informally by Lord Cranston to have nothing to do with it and is told that his involvement might damage his prospects. This warning off quickly raises Kavanagh's hackles and his temper. 'I beg your pardon! What the hell has it got to do with you Laurie, not to put too fine a point on it?' he growls. After a thoughtful walk back to the office, he calls Sarah to offer his help with the appeal without charge.

As work on the appeal continues, the defence team discovers that the murdered woman had been spying on Alan Rainer for the government while posing as his girlfriend. Rainer sold computer encryption programmes to clients who had reason to hide information from the government. The video tape of Rainer killing the young woman was used to blackmail him into revealing the encryption codes. In return, Hatton was framed for the murder.

The case, its various undertones and the interference from Cranston raise doubts in Kavanagh's mind about moving to the bench. 'I'm not sure I want to make people tremble,' he tells Foxcott. 'It is talking *at* people. I'm worried I might miss speaking *for* them.'

Kavanagh receives word that his appointment as a judge has been approved and that he is to be sworn in and immediately assigned a case. He asks for the case to be delayed until after the appeal and is told by Cranston that he either accepts the appointment on the given terms or relinquishes all chance of being offered one again. Kavanagh sticks to his principles and continues with the appeal. He is horrified at the way he is being manipulated by the government through Lord Cranston. It is an attempt to prevent him from uncovering the security service's role in framing Hatton for the murder. 'What's happened to you?' he asks Cranston, having accused him of setting up the urgent timing of the judicial appointment, 'How can you be part of a government that is prepared to let an innocent man stay in prison in order to cover up some cloak and dagger disaster?'

When Kavanagh finally gets Rainer into the witness box, he manages to catch him out in various lies and causes enough doubt and embarrassment that the prosecution, at the instruction of a government representative, drops the case. The appeal is allowed and Hatton is freed, but Rainer and his cohorts also walk away.

The defence team gathers to celebrate in

Kavanagh's office, but while they discuss the case over Champagne, Kavanagh has his back to camera and everyone in the room as he stares out of his office window. The body language is that of a very angry man. The final straw comes when Jeremy Aldermarten, who was counsel for the prosecution in the case, joins the group and claims that he does not regard the result as a loss for him, but rather a victory for justice. 'Balls Jeremy,' Kavanagh turns and growls, 'we none of us won'. So, we fans saw Kavanagh reach the end of his television road on a fighting note.

The appeal of Kavanagh is that at the heart of the character are traits that most of us admire and would like to emulate. Loyalty, honesty, integrity, the courage of one's convictions are all emphasised in the *Kavanagh QC* programmes as qualities to value, even in a world where, as Kavanagh tells Foxcott, their daily task is 'to turn infinite shades of grey into black and white'. That is the joy of television. The characters we get to know and follow can entertain us and perhaps educate us a little, fight battles of conscience for us and be for us what we would like to be. *Kavanagh QC* is a superior programme, which fulfils these functions with satisfyingly rich and complex stories, high production values and consistently fine acting.

Although an able supporting cast surrounds him, it is John Thaw who drives the series. His performances created an ever-likeable, charming and convincing James Kavanagh, a man whose skill and hard work have taken him from humble Manchester working class origins to the top of a tough profession. Kavanagh had a lot in common with John Thaw.

If our hero does not always manage to beat the bad guys, that is okay because we do not tune in to watch Kavanagh win. We tune in to watch John Thaw weave his magic.

John Thaw: an American perspective

by Edna Lief

English specialist, Russianist and educationist, Edna Lief is an adjunct instructor of English at Pace University in Pleasantville, New York. Her English verse translations of the Russian poet Anna Akhmatova are published in the American journal *Tri-Quarterly* and of other Russian poets, including Pushkin, Nekrasov, Pecherin and Ogarev, in *A History of Young Russia*. Edna Lief's translations are also serialised in the journal *Russian History*. She has been interested in mysteries since childhood and early encounters with the novels of Conan Doyle and television dramatisations of them. Like Morse, with whom she feels a particular closeness, she has a passion for art, classical music and crossword puzzles. She lives with her husband, who is a doctor, and has two grown-up children.

Startled, I looked intently at the picture of Inspector Morse, standing beside his vintage Jaguar, peering out from the *New York Times* Obituary page on 23 February, 2002. There must be some mistake. Yes, it was true that the fictional detective had died in Colin Dexter's last Morse mystery novel, *The Remorseful Day*. Only the year before, I had mournfully watched the final episode of *Inspector Morse* on American public television. So what was he doing here among the death notices of real human beings?

Now, I wonder how many American newspaper readers were initially confused, then shocked and saddened to learn that the flesh and blood actor John Thaw had died just as the fictional Morse had done. For me, the loss feels personal. Thaw's outstanding portrayal of the irascible, yet endearing Morse has been part of my psyche since the *Inspector Morse* series was first seen on American public television in 1988. A devoted fan, I have watched every episode – some more than once if they were repeats or if I had recorded them. I also started reading Colin Dexter's novels because of my interest in the television detective and the complicated mysteries that he unravels and eventually solves.

Fact and fiction, reality and illusion. How are we to distinguish them when they seem to intersect so dramatically? As a teacher of English, I remind my university students that literature not only imitates life, but also, ironically, that life imitates literature. The character of Inspector Morse certainly understands this strange blending of art and life when he speaks of opera plots and pontificates to his partner, Sergeant Lewis, about good and evil, life and death, beauty and ugliness, love and hatred, justice and injustice.

Therefore, too, actor John Thaw realised how life and art intersected. On a BBC website, Thaw poignantly discusses his character's death in the final *Inspector Morse* episode, 'Seeing yourself on a mortuary slab pulls you up. I have done a past Morse when he was in hospital and you think that this could be you tomorrow or in six months' time. I could be here as John Thaw.'

We cannot be certain just how much John Thaw was like Morse. According to American television columnist Ron Miller, author of the book *Mystery! A Celebration*, Thaw was proud that Colin Dexter had altered the physical appearance of Inspector Morse in later novels to resemble him. In other interviews with Miller, Thaw compares himself to Morse. He says, 'I love music and I listen to it the way Morse does. It helps me to think, to learn my lines.' He also adds that, like Morse, 'I am an introspective person. I'm not an extrovert.'

Surely, it is Morse's introspective nature and sensitivity to art, poetry, and music which lead him to demand a world of order, not chaos, where right ultimately prevails over wrong? Art, after all, helps us to organise and make sense of disorder and senselessness. After the recent events in New York, the American people turned in astonishing numbers to poetry and music because through them they could express their feelings of grief and loss, anger and acceptance, fear and determination. We Americans sang and recited poems for comfort – both in public and in private. In the same way, Inspector Morse listens to music and recites verse when he needs to reflect on the events of his world and the people in it.

Nevertheless, when Morse flies off at a philosophical tangent, it is Lewis who 'brings him back to earth'. The character of Lewis is a counterbalance for Morse. Lewis keeps Morse centred in the real world of the crime in hand. In addition, he provides the common sense that Morse's intelligence sometimes lacks. Lewis also interprets the words and actions of Morse's intellectual world for us. In the episode, 'Greeks Bearing Gifts', Morse waxes poetic that the people in their murder investigation are like actors in a Greek tragedy. He comments, 'First there is pleasure, then payment. Then there's retribution.' To this, Lewis simply replies, 'My mother used to say laughter always comes to crying'.

More than anything, what distinguishes the character of Inspector Morse is what Colin Dexter calls his 'alpha plus brain'. He is a thinker, an Oxford University educated detective who is a keen observer of people. He tackles murder investigations like cryptic crossword puzzles by examining each clue and filling in the blanks. Frequently, however, Morse is rushing helter-skelter in the wrong direction until he reassesses his clues and connects them correctly. Creators of crossword puzzles say that the way to solve the really difficult ones is to attack each clue fearlessly without worrying about writing in a wrong word. In time, the sharp mind will come at the clue from a different angle and will allow the solver to rewrite it correctly. This is exactly how Morse approaches his work and life.

Ron Miller's last interview with Thaw was entitled 'Interview Case Closed: A Remorseful Interview with John Thaw' for the *Mystery!* website of the Public

Broadcasting Service (PBS). Miller asks the actor if he has to work at depicting Morse's 'subtle yet expressive' qualities. Thaw replies, 'Yes, I give it a lot of time and thought just to make it fresh and subtle and believable. That is my main task really – to make viewers believe that this is a real man with real problems. It is consciously done. I'm not an instinctive actor.'

Time after time, Thaw portrays his character's sensibilities so vividly that the actor seems to embody Inspector Morse. In the documentary, *The Last Morse*, the actress Patricia Hodge explains that sometimes in a scene with Thaw, she wonders if it's 'really John or Morse' she is dealing with. Moreover, Thaw captures the dramatic quality of the role without ever losing control. He uses his piercing blue eyes and facial expressions to great effect.

Certainly, John Thaw's work proves repeatedly that his consciousness as an actor gives his roles credibility with his audiences. Unfortunately, American fans have not seen Thaw in as many television series and programmes as many would like. The *Inspector Morse* series ran on PBS for 13 years from 1988, while the series continues on the Arts and Entertainment cable station (A&E) and BBC America. PBS also ran the historical drama, *Drake's Venture*, which starred Thaw as the explorer Francis Drake, *Into the Blue,* two series of *Kavanagh QC* and *Monsignor Renard*. A&E broadcast the four-part *A Year in Provence*. America also saw Thaw in secondary roles, such as in the dramatisation of the Sherlock Holmes story, *The Sign of Four* and the feature films, *Chaplin, Cry Freedom* and *The Loneliness of the Long Distance Runner.*

It is interesting that, although John Thaw looks perfectly natural and relaxed in jeans and tee shirt in *A Year in Provence*, he isn't quite suited to speak the lines given to the Peter Mayle character he plays. As Mayle, Thaw often has to spout irritating clichés, such as 'Friendship is a lesson in giving'. Even Morse-like sarcasm and the exasperated tone he uses when speaking poor French to eccentric workmen and neighbours does not enliven the mediocre script. Still, Thaw manages to rise above the text. The actor's understanding of Mayle's genial nature allows him to give a watchable and charming performance.

As the polished and successful barrister in *Kavanagh QC*, Thaw's versatility really shows. Like Morse, Kavanagh has a sharp mind and a soft heart. Again, Thaw reveals both attributes in a variety of ways. In court, he speaks authoritatively by using a voice that sounds loud, clear and convincing. During a trial, he often scowls, audibly sighs and smiles in a forced and obligatory way at a judge whom he dislikes. In the episode, 'Job Satisfaction', after Kavanagh has won an appeal for his client, Caroline, she confesses that her brother, who defended himself at trial, is the murderer of their parents. Because Kavanagh realises that Caroline may be her brother's next victim, he alerts the police, even though he has no proof. Of course, his hunch is right and his action saves the day. When his Head of Chambers, Peter Foxcott, calls him a 'vigilante barrister', Kavanagh smiles widely and bellows, 'Bring it on, bring it on!' In the same episode, Kavanagh's father has a stroke and his mother suddenly dies. Appropriately, instead of bravado, Thaw is tender and anguished in the scenes with Kavanagh's parents. His tears are genuine and his performance is persuasive.

As the anti-Nazi French priest in *Monsignor Renard*, John Thaw is a defiant 1940s character with a strong will, clever head and kind heart. Renard is surely cut from the same cloth as Morse, except that the detective finds religion uncomfortable and even instructs his lawyer that he wants no religious service at his death. Like Morse, the priest stands determined to do what is morally right. Therefore, he helps the French Resistance. Renard even has a previous, pre-priesthood love interest that is also reminiscent of Morse.

Since Thaw's death, America's PBS has re-shown the one-off drama *Goodnight, Mister Tom* to much critical acclaim. As Tom Oakley, Thaw skilfully shows what his character is feeling and thinking, often without words. The viewer can sense Oakley's loneliness and hurt from Thaw's eyes before being told of the death of his young wife and child some years earlier. Thaw conveys the old man's scepticism or disapproval with just a raised eyebrow or a glowering glance. In some ways, Tom Oakley, too, resembles Morse because of his keen intelligence and his willingness to break the rules for a just purpose. Oakley snatches the abused boy, Willie, from the care of doctors because he senses that they are doing the boy more harm than good. He calls it rescuing, not kidnapping. Then, reasoning with smaller-minded men, Oakley argues his way into legally adopting Willie.

In the *Inspector Morse* episode, 'Masonic Mysteries', the murderer – Hugo de Vries – has Morse at gunpoint and the detective contemplates in what he believes to be his last moments on earth. John Thaw makes a haunting scene compellingly real by the tightness of his mouth and the anguish and focus in his eyes. Similarly, towards the end of 'The Remorseful Day', Morse, now gravely ill and in obvious pain, slumps in a chair alone at home. On a nearby table, he sees his bird books and the unappealing medicine bottle – symbols of his future life of retirement. His eyes express deep sorrow and the awful acknowledgement of what is ahead. The camera slowly closes in on Thaw's immensely expressive and haggard face. The actor is utterly convincing in these evocative, silent moments on screen.

Now that John Thaw is dead, it is unclear how frequently American public and cable television stations will broadcast his television series and films that already have proven success. One PBS station, WLIW on Long Island, New York, intends to broadcast all 29 episodes of the comedy series *Home To Roost* for the first time in autumn 2002.

During its 'pledge drive' on 17 May, 2002, the broadcasting station held its Second Annual WLIW 21 Battle of the Britcoms. When viewers phoned the network they agreed to join WLIW or to make a donation. They could also vote for one of five British situation comedies: *The Boss*, *Two Point Four Children*, *Home to Roost*, *My Hero* and *Coupling*. During the evening, short promotional clips and a single full-length episode of each show were broadcast. The show to receive the most votes would then be the station's next acquisition for the regular Friday night line-up of British imports. The WLIW website posted a plot summary and the names of the starring actors for each sitcom. Before John Thaw's 1985 sitcom *Home To Roost* was even broadcast, it was ahead in the count. The announcer encouraged viewers by saying, 'Maybe you love John Thaw – tell the phone operator your vote – make a pledge'. The following week, programme manager, Nick Frazer, announced that a majority of viewers had voted for the John Thaw series.

In 'A New Life', the first episode of *Home To Roost,* Thaw is middle-aged divorcé Henry Willows who contentedly lives alone. Suddenly, his teenage son Matthew, whom he has not seen for seven years, appears on the doorstep and asks to stay. At first, Willows refuses, but then warms to his son and agrees to try the arrangement. The differences in their ages and temperaments provide the comic friction. It is curious that here Thaw plays a starchy, solitary man who has a sharp wit and a tongue to match. In some ways, it is like the role of Morse that was to follow.

I watched this first programme with interest.

Thaw produces the same ironic edge that we see in *Inspector Morse*, but there is also slapstick-type physicality as Thaw playfully kicks his son in the rear to show that, as a dad, he will cheerfully discipline his unruly charge. It seems unusual now to see John Thaw being playful and yet he is wholly believable. It is a convincing portrayal of a stern traditionalist who has a less-than-traditional sense of humour.

Therefore, fortunately, American audiences will be able to see more of John Thaw in the near future. Indeed, the publicity department of WLIW reports plans to broadcast a new season of *Kavanagh QC*. On its 1999 'sounding board' (the station's invitation at the end of a broadcast for viewers to call or e-mail with their comments) the station received 54 calls after the second episode of *Kavanagh QC*. An average show gets between 12 and 24. Comments included: 'anything with John Thaw is just great, a programme of high standards', '... we love it as we love *Inspector Morse* ...' 'I have long been a fan of Morse and enjoy his new role in Kavanagh ...' '... one of the best on all of TV'. It is also possible that WLIW will show *Inspector Morse* again since it still holds the rights to the series. In addition, according to the distributor American Public Television (APT), 20 American sta-

tions have opted for the first time to show Thaw's last film *Buried Treasure* sometime in the next few years. APT's fact sheet describes the drama as a 'poignant tale of love and redemption'. Yet, none of *The Sweeney* episodes has appeared on public or commercial television in the United States and it is hoped that station programmers will consider importing them as well.

So clearly, John Thaw – especially as Morse – is tremendously popular among American television critics and the public. Take John J. O'Connor writing in *The New York Times* about the *Inspector Morse* episode, 'The Wolvercote Tongue' which PBS showed on 15 December, 1988. 'And Mr Thaw's Morse is, of course, the best reason for watching,' he declared. He ends his review with, 'Solid, not flashy, Mr Thaw gives the inspector a perfect turn'. *Newsday* critic John Anderson notes in his 2 May, 1990 review of 'The Setting of the Sun' that, 'Thaw's triumph as Morse is making the audience like a man of obvious flaws'.

In his next review, on 10 March, 1988, O'Connor makes some curious observations about viewers' preferences. He begins his review by reminding readers that during pledge week, the PBS station, WNET Channel 13 in New York is '... tailoring its schedule to researcher specifications'. Hence, the poetry series *Voices and Visions* featuring a programme on Emily Dickinson is replaced in its prime time slot by the series *Inspector Morse*. After discussing the two hour-long episodes of the mystery 'Service of All the Dead', O'Connor concludes, 'He is very much worth watching, this Inspector Morse, and I'm sure he would be delighted if everybody stayed tuned to learn something about Emily Dickinson'. How fascinating that John Thaw's British inspector should be a television station's crowd-pleaser and fund-raiser rather than the American poet Emily Dickinson.

Over the years, John Thaw continued to attract many good reviews in America, even when the material was, perhaps, substandard. Although entertainment columnist Sylvie Drake condemns the BBC production of *A Year In Provence* in her 20 March, 1993 column for the *Los Angeles Times*, she applauds John Thaw and his co-star Lindsey Duncan for their 'amiable performances'. Television critic Will Joyner writes in his 2 October, 1997 critique of *Into the Blue* that, 'Despite the drama's uneven pace and "Gothic excess", John Thaw's performance is an "off-kilter tour de force" and a reminder of how much the actor contributes to the success of public television's *Mystery!* series'.

Nevertheless, on 29 January, 2001, *Los Angeles Times* critic Howard Rosenberg reports that PBS is retiring its series *Mystery!* after almost 21 years because of competition from the cable stations A&E and BBC America, who also show British mysteries. In the same article, Rosenberg goes on to announce the broadcasting of the last *Inspector Morse* episode, 'The Remorseful Day'. He laments that John Thaw, 'played Morse so vividly ... that it's been hard accepting him (the actor's nightmare) in other roles'.

For me, *Inspector Morse* is unsurpassable because Colin Dexter's characters, particularly Morse himself, are so finely chiselled and fully sculpted. What makes the character of Morse resonate so deeply with me is that his wounded and melancholy heart responds to art, music, poetry and women. These traits combine with the strong analytical mind, which remains active until he solves his crosswords or resolves his murder investigations and brings the guilty parties to justice. He sees the Greek tragedy of everyday life in the modern Oxford where he lives and works. Nevertheless, isn't every town or city a microcosm of our world where human passions sometimes play out in tragic ways? Morse hates the sight of blood at murder scenes and retches at autopsies because violence and death illuminate peoples' destructive and immoral natures, as well as their vulnerability. He drinks excessively as a means of escape. Real ale is his coping mechanism and the pub his regular refuge.

Each episode of *Inspector Morse* reveals new clues to the detective's real identity so that, eventually, it is Morse himself who becomes the mystery that we want to solve as much as the murder investigation. He is a solitary figure, scarred by female rejection and his long-concealed forename, Endeavour. He can alienate anyone with his apparent indifference and abrasive air of superiority. Yet, he forges a completely credible bond with his younger partner, Lewis. Morse has the ideas and Lewis does the legwork. Morse curtly tells Lewis what to do and Lewis obligingly does it. Morse's senior position is not lost on Lewis, who sometimes grumbles about the unfair amount of time and energy that is required of him. But he always carries out Morse's instructions. Lewis may resist Morse's invitations to out-of-hours sessions at the pub, which he usually ends up paying for, in order to go home to his wife and children. Lewis clearly respects the wisdom of the older, more educated Morse. He recognises that his boss's talents produce results.

Gradually, Morse becomes both a father figure and a teacher to Lewis. The inspector not only instructs his protégé on the use of proper English, but also exposes him to literature, classical music and opera. However, the young sergeant often comically rebuffs Morse's advice on female behaviour. Lewis usually proves to be more astute when it comes to women. Moreover, we sense that Morse envies Lewis his family.

In the episode, 'Greeks Bearing Gifts' the viewer gets a rare glimpse of Lewis's married life. We see him having dinner with his wife at a Greek restaurant. They are both taking Greek lessons and have presumably chosen this restaurant so that they can practise. The scene highlights how different the sergeant's lifestyle is from that of the loveless and solitary Morse. Later, we see Lewis and his closely-knit family watching television together in their cosy home. The Lewises appear to be a very ordinary, late twentieth-century family. In contrast and at the same time, we are shown Morse, pensive and alone, watching a murder investigation video. He had to borrow a television set and VCR from police headquarters because he does not own such equipment. The detective seems old-fashioned and otherworldly. In the same episode, Morse is romantically attracted to the women he meets, such as Lewis's Greek teacher, who is enlisted to help with the case, and a television talk show host, who turns out to be the killer. Lewis, as perfectly played by Kevin Whately, is constantly amused by his partner's weakness for women and shows the audience this with a boyish grin or a knowing glance.

The mutual respect and affection between Morse and Lewis culminates in two emotional acts. The first is when Morse, with his dying breath, asks Superintendent Strange to thank Lewis for him. Apart from the occasional 'well done', Morse never expresses his gratitude to Lewis throughout their long partnership. The second occurs when Lewis reverently kisses the forehead of his dead boss and says, 'Good-bye, Sir'. That kiss demonstrates an emotional attachment that Lewis has never shown to the living Morse.

Professor Robert Klaeger, Chair of the English and Communications Department of Pace University in Pleasantville, New York, suggests that Morse is a romantic hero because he never gives up the chase and doggedly persists, no matter what others say or do. Although continually unlucky in love, Morse nevertheless does not give up his pursuit of the women who find him attractive. In his own gruff way, Morse is genteel, with a gentleman's sensibilities when it comes to women. He accepts their rejection with dignity and dismay. He is never angry and combative towards the women who leave him.

In general, Americans have a romanticised view of England with its gorgeous, rolling landscapes, country estates and beautiful gardens. The Thames Valley scenery of the *Inspector Morse* series reinforces this view and adds to our enjoyment of each episode. Since the show is shot on location, the streets and spires of Oxford are now recognisable to American viewers. How romantic, too, that Morse drives a striking red Mark II Jaguar. American detectives, even on television shows, drive mid-sized Fords of nondescript colour.

Another feature that gives Inspector Morse that romantic edge is the music composed by Barrington Pheloung. The main tune of the Morse code represents the inspector's melancholy. Furthermore, the frequent choir scenes and opera excerpts often provide episodes with additional dramatic tension and emotional punch. A memorable example of this occurs in the episode, 'Promised Land', where the last sequence shows Morse ascending the steps of the magnificent opera house in Sydney, Australia. As usual, he is alone and contemplative. In the background is the waltz music from Richard Strauss's romantic opera, *Der*

Rosenkavalier, in which a gentleman's emissary delivers a silver rose – symbolising love – to a lady. In an interview, John Thaw described this scene as elegiac.

Americans like to see individualism and independence in a character as well as romance. Another characteristic that attracts so many of us to Inspector Morse is his self-confident, renegade spirit. He is willing to buck the system in order to bring a case to its rightful conclusion and that is in the spirit of the American hero who takes pride in a 'can-do, will-do' mentality. Intrinsic to the American Dream is the belief that anything is possible if the individual has a strong will and a creative mind. Unencumbered by the British social class structure, Americans will rebel against an established authority if they believe firmly in a cause or goal. It is something of that spirit that we see in the very first episode of *Inspector Morse*, 'The Dead of Jericho'. Morse illegally breaks into a murder victim's house to look for evidence when he's not officially on the case. He risks the censure of his superiors because he believes that the detective assigned to the case has overlooked important clues, without which the murderer will elude the police.

In the same episode, Superintendent Strange tells Morse that he has been passed over for promotion because he is unorthodox. Indeed, Morse seems to revel in his individualism and independence. He is aware of his uniqueness and wears it almost as a badge of honour. Americans admire and support individuals despite their oddities or flaws. They respect people who break rules and 'think outside the box' in order to succeed in righteous endeavours. We call them heroes.

Pace University professor, Dr Richard Podgorski, who teaches an English seminar on Arthur Conan Doyle's Sherlock Holmes, sees many similarities between Holmes and Morse. Both men are quirky, with idiosyncrasies that make them unique. They are often abrasive and overbearing, but can also be compassionate. Intellectual superiority makes both Holmes and Morse reject authority figures. Both enjoy putting down their subordinate partners, Watson and Lewis. Holmes and Morse are silent about themselves so there is a dark, unknown side to each. They love music – Holmes plays the violin while Morse listens to opera. Holmes claims to use cocaine only when he's bored, to act as a stimulus. Similarly, Morse says he drinks in order to sharpen his thought processes – even when on duty. Both are confirmed bachelors, making them more independent and less likely to listen to others. Although charismatic, Holmes and Morse are both isolated from society.

The big difference between the two fictional detectives is that Inspector Morse is fascinated with women, especially those with their own problems. In turn, they are drawn to him. It is like one wounded person seeking another wounded person. In addition, Morse seems to have the kind of feminine sensibilities and instincts that set him apart from other men.

What seems implausible to Dr Podgorski, a police officer himself for three years, is that Holmes and Morse encounter so many supremely clever adversaries. In reality, although criminals can be complicated, they are usually very stupid. They substitute ruthlessness for intelligence. Also, since art shows us the motivation for an action, Sherlock Holmes and Inspector Morse routinely uncover the reasons why the murderers kill their victims. In real life, people do not always know why they do things. Their motives are not always discernible.

According to Dr Joseph Ryan, Chair of Criminal Justice and Sociology at Pace University, the good detective questions what he sees. He is an excellent observer of human nature who uses instinct, intuition and has good 'internal radar'. He needs well-developed interviewing skills, so that he knows when to use a soft touch and when to get tough. The effective detective is clever and innovative. If he thinks about breaking a rule, he asks himself, 'Does the end justify the means?' The fictional Inspector Morse meets all Dr Ryan's criteria. But in America, good detectives must be good witnesses because they are required to testify so often at trials. I cannot imagine the prickly Morse as an ideal witness. He would probably rub the jury or the judge the wrong way with an arrogant remark or an abstruse literary allusion. Not only that, but Morse would perjure himself if he thought it would serve the interests of true justice. Consider the episode 'Service of All the Dead' in which Morse is untruthful about the actions of his current love interest, Ruth Rawlinson. He wants her to receive a lighter sentence so that she can return home to nurse her ailing mother.

In America, every policeman carries a gun. It is, therefore, essential that law enforcement officers have a strong moral sense. They also need self-control. Certainly, Morse's morality cannot be doubted, but he would be unhappy either owning or firing a gun.

As a member of the New York City police department for 20 years, three of them as an undercover detective, Dr Ryan understands why so many police officers drink heavily. He recognises their need to anaesthetise themselves and become detached from the everyday danger and violence of the job. He thinks that police work is not conducive to family life. In fact, a detective's life can feel very lonely, even when there are loved ones at home. Surely Inspector Morse's drinking and loneliness fit this profile? Furthermore, only police officers can understand and truly empathise with other police officers. That is why they are ideal drinking or social companions for one another.

Policemen and detectives have to work in pairs so that they can back each up another in dangerous situations. Each can also verify the other's story. Since time is a crucial factor in police work, two officers can accomplish twice as much as one in the same time. Only in small towns or villages, where the budgets are very restricted, does an American police officer or detective work alone. Dr Ryan believes that, in real life, the pairing of an older, more experienced, detective with a younger, less experienced one makes sense. It is also preferable to combine people who are more different than similar as long as they are compatible. They complement and feed off one another.

Hence the success of the fictional symbiotic partnership of Chief Inspector Morse and Detective Sergeant Lewis.

Although my university colleagues know and admire the work of John Thaw, my students do not. In America, John Thaw is not a household name. Baby Boomers and Senior Citizens may be watching dramas and mysteries on television, but Generations X and Y choose 'reality' shows. The enormous success in 2002 of the *Ozzy Osbourne* show on the cable channel MTV tells its own story. Millions of viewers have been tuning in each week to watch Ozzy and his family who, natural and unscripted, interact with their dogs and cats, their friends and each other in their posh Beverly Hills, California home. When I asked the 14-year-old who works at a local bakery if he knew who John Thaw was, he was blank. But he is a fan of the *Ozzy Osbourne* show, not because he likes the British rock star's music, but because, he says, it is fun to see that Ozzy's family is not so different from his family after all. Even though Ozzy is an outrageous and wealthy rock star, he's also a caring dad who yells as much as his own father does.

Chris, a 26-year-old electrician, has never heard of John Thaw. But he and his girlfriend watch the

American police dramas *NYPD Blue* and *Law and Order*, whose non-stop action and fast pace are very different from the leisurely tempo of *Inspector Morse*. They are also fans of *ER*, the highly popular and long running hospital series about life in a fictional metropolitan hospital emergency room. His father, Chris said, is the one who likes American and British television mysteries.

Nevertheless, there are young Americans who are great fans of John Thaw's Inspector Morse. Anne Guerry, a 28-year old PhD candidate in zoology and marine biology at Oregon State University, and 31-year old Joshua Lawler, who has his PhD in ecology and does conservational planning for United States Environmental Protection Agency, have created their own game to play when they watch videotaped episodes of *Inspector Morse.* Whoever first identifies the murderer, gets five points. The first to guess Morse's love interest earns two points and the first to spot the author Colin Dexter gains one point. The person with the most points at the end of the episode is the winner.

Josh started watching television mysteries with his parents when he was a teenager. He began watching the *Inspector Morse* series in college and was 'hooked'

by the Morse character and the complicated plots. Josh, whose parents recently gave him the entire set of Inspector Morse videos, introduced Anne to Morse. Therefore, he and Anne are now viewing each episode again in sequence. What attracts Josh to Morse's character is that, although he is very intelligent and has studied at the University of Oxford, Morse rejected a stuffy academic career. Rather, as a detective, he is doing something socially useful – unlike the Oxford dons after whom he is often chasing.

Josh also admires Morse's – often-scientific – scepticism. The detective approaches cases like scientific puzzles. He envies Morse the speed with which he develops clues and solves cases. It contrasts with the slowness of setting up ecological experiments. Further, Josh respects Morse for being able freely to admit to being wrong or being stumped. On the other hand, Morse can be sexist even though he likes women so much. The inspector is quite taken aback when the female pathologist Dr Russell suddenly replaces the familiar pathologist Max. Whenever she appears, there is verbal sparring between her and Morse.

Because, in his professional life Josh spends so much time using a computer, he finds it 'classy' that

Morse rejects computers. It is certainly true that, although occasionally Morse prompts Lewis to access computer information vital to a case, he always relies on his own brain, rather than a big database, to make the crucial, mystery-solving connections.

What Anne finds frustrating about Morse's character are his many unsuccessful relationships with women and his constant drinking, which seems to be part of the fabric of Oxford life. In the episode 'The Last Enemy', Morse drinks to numb the discomfort of toothache. This use of alcohol might be a way for Morse to blot out the emotionally painful part of his life.

To Anne, *Inspector Morse* is impressive because it is not formulaic in the way so many American detective shows are. Each story seems fresh and its complexity requires the viewer to think. For her, it is hard to separate the actor John Thaw from his character of Inspector Morse because, she says, 'He never appears to be acting'. She describes his technique as seamless.

Perhaps if John Thaw had sung in a famous rock group or starred in feature-length films, many more Americans – of any age – would know his name. People now recognise Jim Broadbent, the English actor who won the 2002 Oscar for his role in *Iris* with Dame Judi Dench. We also saw him co-star with Nicole Kidman in the 2002 Oscar nominated picture, *Moulin Rouge*. Thaw's fictional wife in *A Year In Provence*, Lindsey Duncan, won the 2002 Tony award for her role in Noel Coward's *Private Lives* that was imported from London to the New York stage. Now she has more name-recognition here. If only John Thaw had starred in a feature film or acted on the New York stage, his fans would be legion.

BBC web-board messages about Thaw come from all over the United States. A viewer from Indianapolis, Indiana comments, 'Many Americans think of British actors as very mannered or elitist. John Thaw reflected in his acting style a more approachable Brit, one who shared attributes of the modern middle-class but with a British twist. Through Inspector Morse, a very popular character among certain Americans, we see a man who is not elitist, but very well educated and self-motivated. He exuded a trait that is not often communicated from the UK to the US – a self-made man who is tough by trade, trying to adapt in a rapidly changing British world.'

Another admirer from Omaha, Nebraska writes, 'I am truly saddened to hear of John Thaw's passing. He was a superb actor of immense talent. I was never lucky enough to meet Mr Thaw in person, but his portrayal of Inspector Morse brought Colin Dexter's book(s) into vivid reality and I will always treasure them. Mr Thaw's portrayal of Morse was sincere and heartfelt. He seemed to have an innate understanding of the character. Both he and Oxford shined as co-stars. My deepest condolences to Mr Thaw's family and friends, he will be truly missed.'

From Atlanta, Georgia, a fan writes, 'Enjoyed the series *Inspector Morse*, John Thaw was perfect for the part and hope it will be shown over here for a long time'.

Even if American television stations eventually stop showing the *Inspector Morse* mysteries, we can still see them on video. My own public library, which serves a community of over 60,000 people who either live or work in this suburb north of New York City, owns 28 videos in which John Thaw appears. These include such diverse films as the documentary, *WWII, The Lost Colour Archives* in which Thaw is the narrator and the Sherlock Holmes episode, *The Sign of Four*. The library also stocks many episodes of *Kavanagh QC*, all the episodes of *A Year in Provence* and the film *Goodnight Mister Tom*. It has most of the *Inspector Morse* series, which are extremely popular,

judging from the library's circulation records. In fact, many of the John Thaw videos are lent out every week on a non-stop basis. The most popular of all the *Inspector Morse* videos are 'Absolute Conviction', 'Setting of the Sun' and 'Last Bus To Woodstock', which the library has owned since 1993. These have all been borrowed many hundreds of times.

It was with the help of the library's assistant director that I learned of Thaw's enormous video circulation record. After we had checked the actual number, she was so impressed that she confided to me that she was definitely going to try the videos herself. It seems that, although she knew the name John Thaw and the novels of Colin Dexter – which are also library favourites – she had never seen any of Thaw's performances.

Although in America we do not have an Inspector Morse Society, as there is in Britain, or even an official John Thaw fan club, we do have a significant number of television viewers who admire the actor and his work and who will continue to want to see it. He has contributed so much to the quality of American television with his stellar performances in productions of superior quality. It seems important that when we spend time watching television, we feel it is time well spent. When

John Thaw is in a film, we can anticipate not only an enjoyable experience, but also a satisfying one.

In an interview with John Koch of the *Boston Globe*, Rebecca Eaton, executive producer since 1985 of the PBS series *Masterpiece Theatre* and *Mystery!* shares her view of television programming today. She explains, 'There is too much television on television, and it is too fast, and it is too shallow. In an age of reality television, of public affairs television, of news coverage and even of excellent documentaries, in contemporary culture there is even more of a need for fiction. Good dramatisation can deliver news about life and about the human condition in a way that you can tolerate better at the end of a hard day, and possibly in a deeper way and a less painful way.'

It is exactly because art exposes the reality of the human condition in a safe and pleasurable way that so many of us love literature and drama. Art allows us to experience life in new ways that give us fresh insight into other people and ourselves.

John Thaw's skill as an actor lay in his profound ability fully to understand the lives of his characters and to portray them vividly and believably. In breathing life into fictional characters, he showed us people with recognisably universal virtues and vices. Art and life intertwined when John Thaw acted. Yes, he entertains us, but his performances always also teach us something about life and may even help us to live it better.

Swansongs

by Ian Wylie

Tyneside-born Ian Wylie is the resident London and Television Editor of the *Manchester Evening News*, one of Britain's largest regional evening newspapers. He has been a senior journalist for 25 years and has reported many major events, including the wedding of Prince Charles and Lady Diana Spencer at St Paul's Cathedral and the funerals of Diana, Princess of Wales and the Queen Mother at Westminster Abbey. The numerous cases Ian Wylie has profiled at London's Old Bailey include the trial of the Yorkshire Ripper and many high-profile hearings at the High Court and Appeal Court. As a member of the Parliamentary Press Lobby, he has covered several General Election campaigns. During the last 20 years, he has interviewed hundreds of film and television stars, including Dustin Hoffman, Albert Finney, Tom Courtenay, Kevin Whately, Dennis Waterman, Joanna Lumley, John Nettles and David Jason. Ian Wylie lives in London with his wife, daughter and tennis racket.

John Thaw would have smiled at the tributes paid to him after his death. The Manchester-born star, who rose from a humble background and broken home to become Britain's most popular actor, was a shy and modest man.

We last met just a few weeks before the diagnosis of the cancer that was to claim his life, one of many interviews over the last 15 years. Now white-haired, John blushed when told that co-star Sarah Lancashire had described him as a national treasure. Yet, that is exactly what he was. An always polite, quiet, gentle man, with a dry sense of humour and just an edge of gritty cop Jack Regan's cynicism in *The Sweeney*, he would recall stories from bygone television days and chuckle at the memories. He was a firm favourite with the press because he had no starry pretentiousness. However, watch the recordings of the awards ceremonies he was persuaded to attend and you will see an uneasy and wary Thaw, who found it difficult to understand his status as the nation's favourite television actor. Fame was the downside of the profession he loved.

In 1993, I interviewed John about his forthcoming starring role in *A Year In Provence*. Days later, he dutifully appeared for a second interview about yet another television project. In addition, on the Saturday morning in between, I watched as Thaw and actress wife Sheila Hancock tried to avoid all glances as they did their shopping in our local supermarket. Being as famous as John Thaw was not always easy. He was always on his guard for an ambush next to the frozen peas. 'My heart sinks when I arrive in the car park because you do get stared at. People say things like: "I know I shouldn't do this, but will you sign this?" Or: "It is, isn't it? I know you want to be private but will you sign these four checkout slips?" I've signed anything from bus tickets to backs of cigarette packets.'

In May 1999, he appeared in *Plastic Man*, a two-part drama about a plastic surgeon, which included scenes filmed at Hillingdon Hospital in Middlesex. Co-star Frances Barber, who played John's mistress, had a different story to tell about John. 'There were some very ill patients around and we took that very seriously,' she explained. 'And, of course, John is probably the most recognisable man in the country. He was incredibly kind to a very sad, poor patient who was bereaved. She couldn't believe it was him – it is a bit of a shock, isn't it, to see John Thaw out of context? It was very moving. She was just very distressed and he took a great deal of time to be nice to her.'

The story illustrates one of the reasons why Thaw was one of our favourite television stars. His acting ability was unquestioned, but, whoever he was playing on screen, John was a man whom his audience loved and trusted. It is not surprising that people wanted their own small piece of him, even if it was written on a pack of petits pois.

For many, John will be remembered simply as Morse, the Oxford detective killed off by a heart attack after solving his thirty-third and last case. Thaw had already confronted his own mortality while lying on a mortuary slab at St Peter's Hospital in Chertsey, Surrey, where the Inspector's final scene was filmed. He told me, 'Throughout the filming of the whole episode, because he is ill right from the beginning, I began to feel unwell in myself. Before each scene, you have to say to yourself "Remember you're ill." He is literally a week or two away from death. Therefore, you have to show that. Moreover, I used to go home and I used to feel unwell. I swear to you I definitely felt unwell during the filming,' he added.

'You've had the best years of my life,' he told his co-star, Kevin Whately, at the last Morse press launch in October 2000. He also shared many a joke with James – Jimmy – Grout, the actor who played his long-suffering boss Chief Superintendent Strange. Although Morse often provoked Strange to the point of exasperation, the two men were good friends off screen.

John found himself back at the scene of Morse's television death while filming what was to be his last *Kavanagh QC* film, 'The End Of Law'. However, this time John, as Kavanagh, was just visiting St Peter's Hospital. 'I have to say it was strange to find myself fit and well, and back where I'd "died" earlier in the year, especially after all the media attention that Morse's death got.'

James Kavanagh was the second long-running role of his later career and the first episode was screened on 3 January, 1995, John's fifty-third birthday. It was decided to make the barrister a character from the north of England. John told executive producer Ted Childs, 'If Manchester is good enough for me, it will be good enough for Kavanagh'. He later placed the character as originally coming from Bolton, but always felt that the lawyer was closer to home. 'In my mind's eye, he originates from Longsight.'

A 1998 episode of *Kavanagh QC* starred his old friend Tom Courtenay in a guest role as murder suspect Dr Felix Crawley, who was accused of poisoning his wife. The two actors had once shared a maisonette in Highbury, north London, when Tom was making his debut at the Old Vic and John was back in the capital from regional rep in Liverpool. 'It was like we'd never ... I was going to say, like we'd never split up,' said Thaw, 'but I don't want you to take that the wrong way. I hadn't seen him for eight or ten years – maybe longer.' Tom also enjoyed the reunion. 'Fairly soon after we had shared the place in London, it was obvious that John was going to be much more of a television actor than I was. I've no regrets about that, and must admit I'm not much of a television watcher.'

Another episode in that year's series featured a case set in Bolton. 'But we filmed it in Longsight, where I was born. The house I grew up in had been pulled down, but we filmed in a high-rise block just ten minutes from there.' A modern housing development now stands on the site of his old home. 'I drove around but I didn't stop the car and knock on any doors. I'd have been told to get lost if I had.'

One day, John received an official letter calling him for jury service. You could just picture the defendant's face, walking into the dock to see Inspector Morse, Kavanagh QC and Regan from *The Sweeney* looking on in judgement. 'I would have done it if required,' Thaw pleaded in mitigation. 'But I think the defence might have something to say, don't you, if they saw me sitting in the front row of the jury box? I might be seen as being a little biased in favour of the law.'

While Morse – and to a lesser extent Kavanagh – were the two defining characters of John's later television career, he took several other small screen roles in the last decade of his life which further cemented his reputation as a viewers' favourite.

They saw a very different Thaw in ITV's two-hour film adaptation of Michelle Magorian's award-winning 1981 novel *Goodnight Mister Tom*, the touching story of a young boy evacuated to the country to avoid the terrors of Blitz-torn London. One of John's most successful single dramas, it won several awards of its own and a special place in many people's hearts. The wartime tale attracted an audience of over 14 million when it was first screened in 1998, making it Britain's highest rated single drama for that year.

John made every effort to impress as organ-playing Tom Oakley, the seemingly simple and gruff white-haired widower forced to take in evacuee Willie Beech. There was no trace of Morse or Kavanagh, once Thaw had perfected his Suffolk-Essex accent. 'Was it a difficult acting job?' I asked him. 'Yes, it was, actually. We had a very good dialect coach and I had a couple of sessions with him before we started filming. I also had a tape that he made, so I used to play that in the car whenever I was travelling. And he was on set all the time.'

The full beard required for the character took some two months to grow, but did not fool fans in the street. 'Maybe people had to look twice – is that John Thaw? I found people staring a little harder than they would normally. But when I finally shaved it off, I felt naked.'

Twelve-year-old schoolboy Nick Robinson played Willie in what was essentially a moving, sensitive and valuable story about living with loss. The book had won the Guardian Children's Fiction Award and it was clear from the first preview screening that the television version was going to provide Thaw with one of his biggest hits.

Actress and author, Michelle Magorian, was appearing in *Joseph and the Amazing Technicolour Dreamcoat* when she first thought up the two central characters. Prompted by the stage show, she sought inspiration in colours, and came up with green and brown – oak and beech. Curmudgeon is the colourful word that springs to mind when we first set eyes on Mr Tom on the day war is declared. Six months later, the arrival in his Suffolk village of a group of children from London's East End changes his life. Under the care of Tom Oakley, young Willie Beech thrives. Thaw's memorable line to officials who want to take 'his' lad away is, 'What the boy needs is love'.

The location for filming was the same Buckinghamshire village and church as that used by the BBC for the Dawn French comedy series *Vicar of Dibley*. It was a setting which complemented an absorbing, old-fashioned story.

'It's nice to do something different,' admitted Thaw. 'Tom's a plain man, not particularly well educated. He is the opposite of somebody like Morse or Kavanagh, but unaffected by that. He lives on his instincts, whereas the other two use their intellect. I suppose I am closer to Tom because I am not a particularly well-educated person myself. I have to rely on my instinct.'

The on-screen relationship between the oak and the beech was, obviously, a key factor in the drama. Thaw made a natural grandfather figure. 'Yes, I got on well with him. Willie's a shy boy by nature, I think, and you want to make sure he's all right, look after him and protect him.'

John's wife, Sheila Hancock, was evacuated from London twice during the war and she helped with his research, telling her husband how much she hated her wartime experience. 'There were lots of problems between the city and country children and a lot of bullying and violence at school,' he explained.

Born in 1942, Thaw had no real memory of those dark days. 'I was too young, to be honest. The only thing that I can remember vividly is when the war ended, the street parties and everybody being very happy and behaving unlike adults had behaved before that. I remember everybody being slightly mad.'

John narrated two ITV documentary series: *The Second World War In Colour* and *Britain At War In Colour*, the latter screened in 2000. The trailers for the programmes explained their appeal. 'War is never black and white.' The freshly assembled colour material, never before seen on television, made a deep impression on John. 'To see shots of Hitler in colour like that. It looks like it was from last year's news, as opposed to 60 years ago. It made me ask myself how could it happen? How could human beings do this? There's lots of footage of Russian and French prisoners-of-war and refugees with horses and carts, which immediately reminds you of the material we've seen this year from Kosovo,' he said.

It also reminded many of his £6 million, four-part drama series *Monsignor Renard*. John starred in the title role as a Catholic priest who, after an absence of 20 years, returns in May 1940 to the French town of his birth just as invading German troops are about to arrive. When John attended the launch of the series at the British Academy of Film and Television Arts in London in March 2000, it was obvious that he was not happy. The reason soon became clear. That same week he had signed a new deal – reported to be worth £2.5 million – with Carlton Television, making him the highest paid television actor in Britain. However, recent events had also led to him holding talks about a possible move to the BBC. 'What changed my mind? It was an offer I could not refuse,' he smiled.

The smile left his face as he explained how television executives had already axed *Monsignor Renard* before a single minute had been seen on screen. After filming in northern France over five summer months the year before, the plan had been to make four more series, taking the priest's story through to the end of the war. Then, just before Christmas, the stunned cast was told that there would be no return for Renard. Carlton had decided the drama was just too expensive to produce.

Thaw believed that, in Renard, he had found a new

long-running character to move on to from Morse and Kavanagh. 'When you know what went into something, and what you intended it to be is actually what it is, then you can feel very pleased.' He was, as ever, diplomatic about the show's cancellation, restricting his comments to, 'I was disappointed when I was told. A lot of work has gone into it and I think we should all be proud of it. It's a quality drama, but I'm a big boy and that's the way the business goes.'

Co-star Juliette Caton, who played a young French woman called Hélène, was less constrained. 'It's absolutely incredible and something has to be done.' Producer Chris Kelly also saw the character as perfect for John and could not understand the logic behind the move to deny viewers further episodes of what could have been an epic series.

Most filming days saw a swastika unfurled from the town hall in the St Valéry-sur-Somme location, while shop windows were filled with wartime provisions. The sight of German uniforms also brought back memories. 'Some of the older people watching us, or living in the town, had been through it all. Inevitably, it opened old wounds. I admit I felt humbled,' said John. The clothes he wore for Augustin Renard's services actually belonged to the church of St Martin, which dominated the main square of the old town. 'They were very old and had been worn by many different priests. I was aware as I stood in the pulpit talking to the congregation that the vestments could well have been worn in that pulpit in 1940.'

A year later, he was still musing over the fate of the series. 'Dare I say it, but everyone I meet, when *Monsignor Renard* comes up, says how much they enjoyed it. They were looking forward to it going on. The TV people spent months getting all the clothes and props together, and now it's all been sold off.'

For the 1999 two-part thriller, *The Waiting Time*, based on the novel by Gerald Seymour, Thaw had turned Teutonic himself. He played solicitor's clerk Joshua Mantle, a lonely man who becomes involved in a chilling post-Cold War adventure. It was filmed in the thick of a north German winter. John said, 'I had never been so cold in my life. We were literally at the sea's edge with the wind coming off the Baltic. It felt like it was going right through you. One member of the crew got frostbite in the ears. Within three days, I got a very bad cold. I wore a vest, which I don't normally wear, and two layers of thermals under my costume of shirt, jumper, car coat and a scarf – and even then I was still cold.'

The first episode saw Thaw scrambling over Berlin rooftops in a throwback to his Sweeney-style action days. 'I was attracted by Gerald Seymour's novel, which I read before it was even published, and said yes before I saw a script. One of the attractions of playing Mantle is that it is a new role, not some old war-horse I have done before.' He also had to speak fluent German. 'Initially, I was very nervous in front of the German crew. A couple of them made suggestions – and once I got my confidence, they were fine.'

Plastic Man had been shown a few months earlier. John took on his first medical role as plastic surgeon, Joe MacConnell, in a moral tale about a man who appears to have got what he wanted in life – successful career, loving wife, children and 'colour supplement home' – but none of that stops him straying into an affair with an attractive colleague, played by Ms Barber. It also featured him 'getting his kit off', although the scene was very discreet. 'You do not actually seeing them making love or anything. It's post-coital,' he stressed. 'You're always a bit nervous getting into bed but everybody, in my experience, makes jokes or tries to lighten the atmosphere.' Thaw and Barber's lips had, of course, met on screen before,

when he was Inspector Morse and she was his opera-singing idol in 'The Death of The Self'.

The 1997 single drama *Into the Blue* also involved bed. John was playing alongside young actress Abigail Cruttenden, real-life partner of *Sharpe* star Sean Bean. 'I didn't actually share a bed,' he protested. 'The director Jack Gold was very clever in the way he staged that – I don't want Sean chasing me!'

The two-hour thriller was partly shot on the Greek island of Rhodes in a plot linked to a Manchester express train. John's character was called Harry Barnett, a bankrupt former wealthy garage owner employed on the island as a caretaker. Barnett spends the night with a young Englishwoman, Heather, played by Abigail, then she vanishes. Harry is arrested on suspicion of murder. Part of *Into the Blue* was filmed in Cambridge. So, it provided a bit of redress for the Cambridge tourism authority, Oxford having benefited from *Inspector Morse* for so long.

In later years, John did not seek roles in feature films, pointing out that his television dramas were made to cinema standards. They just happened to be shown on a smaller screen. 'I would sooner do leading parts on television than have ten minutes over 20 weeks in a so-called Hollywood blockbuster.'

Although his instincts in choosing projects were usually reliable, *A Year in Provence* proved to be one of his few ratings failures at home in Britain. John Thaw and Sheila Hancock had bought their home in Provence some two-and-a-half years before he started work on the series. It provided the perfect retreat from the pressures of fame back in England and was, by complete coincidence, not far from the television location. Mr and Mrs Thaw discovered the area when John's actress daughter, Abigail, had stayed there while filming an episode of BBC's *Bergerac* and was visited by her mum, Sheila. 'We just fell in love with the area and ended up buying a house.'

The Sweeney and *Inspector Morse* were both shown in France, but there was little chance of the veteran actor being mobbed in the local supermarket. 'There are a few people who have seen Morse, not many. That is mainly because it was on at Sunday lunchtimes. Fortunately, our house cannot be seen from the road. Nobody knows it exists.' It was only later that John read Peter Mayle's best-selling book which, he stressed, did not influence his own property purchase. 'It certainly didn't put me off, but I'm not about to buy a house because I've read a book.'

Filming the role of former advertising, executive Mayle, alongside Lindsay Duncan as his wife Jenny, left little time for relaxation. 'I have not worked so hard for years. It was six days a week, 12 hours a day.'

John and Sheila returned many times to their French home. 'We only go to France together. I don't go on my own because she speaks better French than I do.' Provence also provided an escape from public gaze after the announcement that he was suffering from cancer of the oesophagus. John had once been a heavy smoker. Both his parents had died of cancer. The same disease was to take John's own life all too swiftly. He had asked for privacy while being treated for an illness with a bleak recovery rate. He got it. Sheila, who had herself beaten breast cancer 13 years previously, smiled and remained optimistic at a later television event. However, she confessed, 'It's not been easy. We've had a tough year.'

Hopes for John's recovery were raised when he made his first public appearance since his treatment. He appeared at a November 2001 Buckingham Palace reception for the broadcasting industry hosted by the Queen. Dressed in black tie and dinner jacket, he arrived early and ran up the stairs, avoiding most of the limelight surrounding the event.

He was still fighting cancer when his final television appearance was screened. Filmed some 18 months earlier, *Buried Treasure* found John playing a Manchester estate agent. His co-star was child actress Dominique Jackson. He returned to his roots to play widower Harry Jenkins, a devious and selfish man with a big house in Cheshire. He cheats at golf and much else besides, but, unlike Morse and Kavanagh, this was a character who was not in control. One day Harry returns home from the golf club to find two young police officers waiting for him. His pursuit of profit is interrupted when they tell him that Annie, the estranged daughter he has not seen for ten years, has been killed in a car crash. Then he discovers he is grandfather to a little girl called Saffron. She is a mixed race child. Until now he had not known of her existence.

'He's a self-absorbed businessman,' explained John. 'His first thought is "How is this going to affect me?" Reluctantly, he takes the youngster in. She turns his life upside down, which reminds him that winning isn't everything.'

A montage sequence saw John and his screen granddaughter on a joyful tourist tour taking in the sights of London including Tower Bridge, Trafalgar Square and Big Ben. There was also a trip on the London Eye, where Saffron tap-danced high above the Thames. Although the television crew had booked a capsule in advance, much of what is seen on screen was improvised. 'When we turned up and there was this big queue, they rushed us to the front and let us on because we had the cameras and the lights and all the heavy equipment. It was great fun. I really enjoyed it,' smiled John. At the end of their day, Thaw, as Harry, entered lullaby land, singing *All My Loving* by the Beatles to sleepy Saffron. 'It's not something I'm known for,' he acknowledged. 'I once sang with a choir as Morse and once with Dennis Waterman on *The Sweeney*, but on that occasion we were supposed to be drunk. It was a song that was recorded by Bing Crosby and Jimmy Durante and it was called *The Song's Gotta Come From The Heart*,' he recalled, before bursting into his best Durante impression.

Dominique, just eight at the time of filming, had never heard of John's favourite group the Rolling Stones and asked him if the Beatles were 'from the old days'. The Manchester schoolgirl also confessed that, at first, the name of her veteran co-star meant nothing to her. 'My mum had told me he was Inspector Morse and quite famous, but I didn't know him. I think my mum was more nervous of meeting him than I was. He felt like a real granddad.'

Proud family man Thaw, with three grandchildren of his own, was anxious to give credit to his co-star. 'She was word perfect. I believe they've got a clip where I dried and she told me my line, just like that.' When the cameras weren't rolling, John and Dominique would serenade each other with their own unique versions of Tom Jones's *Sex Bomb*.

He clearly enjoyed making *Buried Treasure* but dismissed comparisons with *Goodnight Mister Tom*. 'Yes, that was also about a man and a child but as characters they are quite different. They are single, selfish, self-centred people at the start of the films, but I think there the comparisons end. *Buried Treasure* has some funny lines, which I have not done for a while on TV. I thought I'd remind the audience that I've got a sense of humour, something I think Tom Oakley was probably a bit short of.

'It is a feel-good story. The writer Peter Bowker had written my part in exactly the right rhythms from how I remember the way Mancunians talk. Coming from Manchester, as I do, I loved doing the accent. It was just easy to slip back into that rhythm of speech. Nevertheless, my original Manchester accent was much thicker than Harry's was when I first started in RADA. That was why you went to RADA, to lose that accent, because otherwise you wouldn't get work in those days. I do not regret it at all. If you get a so-called standard English accent, then you have laid the basis for any other accents that you might want to do. I, obviously, go up to Manchester to work occasionally, and I used to go up to see my dad, who is sadly gone. So I just put my thinking cap on to remember what guys like Harry talk like.'

Although it was his last drama to be screened on British television, *Buried Treasure* was not John's final television project. Harry and Saffron's tale was taken out of its original slot, held back by the schedulers and screened out of sequence, after Thaw's performance in *The Glass*, a serial he actually began filming on 10 October, 2000, the day after the press launch for the farewell Morse programme. *Buried Treasure* was filmed the previous spring.

The six episodes of *The Glass* saw him paired with actress Sarah Lancashire, the one-time *Coronation Street* star who went on to acclaim in a series of ITV dramas, including the award-winning *Seeing Red*. In typically generous fashion, he recognised her talent. 'I think she is one of the most professional actors I have ever worked with, no question. It was a pleasure to work with her, it really was.'

The Glass was billed as 'a story of love, lust and betrayal'. Thaw's character was Jim Proctor, a ruthless self-made millionaire and expert salesman intent on retiring from his double-glazing empire. Sarah played his younger girlfriend, Carol Parker, one of the sales staff. His opening line was 'Shut it,' an in-joke harking back to *The Sweeney*. 'They obviously put that in deliberately. But, as far as I was concerned, it was just the first line of the script.' Moreover, unlike a certain Oxford detective, Proctor was a man who absolutely hated opera. Viewers also got to see John dancing. 'I was deeply embarrassed at the time. I'm turning into an ageing rocker,' he confessed.

In his last interview, at the Royal Society of Arts in central London in May 2001, John said he had no plans to retire. But, on that occasion, he did share his feelings about what lay ahead, should he ever be obliged to stop working. 'I would fill my time reading and walking, going to shows, opera, concerts, sitting in the sun and leisurely lunches. I can think of lots of nice things to do.'

In any event, he was about to take a break from filming. 'I've made a conscious decision to slow down a bit. So that's what I'm doing this year. I'm not working hard, I won't work for a couple of months now, quite deliberately. I shall be doing a one-off film for ITV in the summer, but I do not think I am allowed to tell you about it yet because it has not been given the go-ahead. But it will be.'

A few weeks later an emotional John Thaw collected a valued BAFTA Fellowship from his old friend Sir Tom Courtenay, commenting, 'It's really, truly, one of the happiest moments of my professional life.'

Just 46 days after that last interview, the son of a Manchester lorry driver revealed he was undergoing treatment for cancer. He had every intention of returning to work to make that film for ITV – and many more. Scripts were written for him to begin work on another *Kavanagh QC* film. Sadly, the script of his real life drama was to end in death just eight months after his illness was first made public. He had no inkling that the end was so near and had signed a new year-long contract with ITV the day before he died.

Exactly two months after her husband's death, Sheila Hancock, accompanied by Dominique Jackson, accepted yet another BAFTA on his behalf – the Lew Grade Audience Award, won by *Buried Treasure*. Reflecting after the ceremony, she thanked all those viewers who had voted. 'I think his is a remarkable story. He overcame adversity and fought a lot of personal demons to get where he was. John was really a very shy man who only ever regarded himself as a working actor. Having reached a lovely tranquil stage in his life, he has been snatched away from us. We really do miss him terribly.'

The sun was setting in a winter sky when, as an ill Inspector Morse, John sat in a riverside pub garden finishing his pint of real ale, quoting an extract from an A. E. Housman poem, a line of which gave the final Morse mystery its title – 'The Remorseful Day.'

> Ensanguining the skies
> How heavily it dies
>> Into the west away;
> Past touch and sight and sound,
> Not further to be found,
> How hopeless under ground
>> Falls the remorseful day.

I asked him what his feelings had been as he watched the finished tape alone at home. 'At the end I was choked up, to say the least. That last panning shot across the roofs of Oxford just beautifully finished it for me. It was a very moving little film.'

He later described how he had been overwhelmed by the public's response when the film was transmitted. 'I was aware that it was the end of an era and that something that had gone on for so long was still, at the end, held in – dare I say – great affection by the majority of the public. They were sad to see him disappear. And I thought, well, I'm proud to have been a part of that.

'I went to a screening where they invited all the directors, writers and actors right from the word go. And it was an amazing turnout. People I had not seen for ten years came to, as it were, pay their last respects to it. I was very touched.'

John was not in his profession for the famous face and awards. 'I have always thought of acting as a very serious business,' he once explained. 'If you ask anyone who has worked with me, they will tell you that I carry the script around with me like my last will and testament.'

Thanks to television repeats, Thaw's talent will live on. But for all those who knew him and the millions who thought of him as a friend, the early morning mist over Oxford's dreaming spires will be forever just that little bit thicker.

Appendix

Cancer of the oesophagus – the disease that killed John Thaw

by James Elder

Professor James Elder was born in 1938 in Glasgow, Scotland, where he both went to school and studied medicine at the University. A successful medical career led him to become Senior Lecturer in Surgery and Honorary Consultant Surgeon to the University of Manchester, Department of Surgery at the Manchester Royal Infirmary in 1971. He proceeded to Readership in 1976, pursuing interests in gastric and oesophageal cancer, gastro-intestinal hormones and studies in models of gastric cancer. Since that time, he has maintained this research interest in cancers of the oesophagus and stomach. He was appointed to the first chair in surgery at the School of Postgraduate Medicine at Keele University in 1983. He is the author of over 200 papers and articles on gastro-intestinal disease. He sits on numerous committees and bodies both in Britain and internationally and has been External Examiner in Surgery in a number of universities in the United Kingdom and Hong Kong. He married Sheena in 1964. They have three daughters and four grandchildren. His hobbies are reading, listening to classical music, fly fishing, watching some television, photography, travelling, learning French and wine tasting.

John Thaw suffered from cancer of the oesophagus and, according to press reports, died from causes connected with it in February 2002. Naturally, I cannot comment on his case specifically because he wasn't my patient and, even if he had been, his medical details would be confidential. So what follows is a general account of this devastating disease.

The oesophagus, or gullet, is the tube which connects the throat to the stomach. It encounters all the liquid and solid substances we swallow and interacts with the natural and processed molecules in our food. So it is in regular contact with much of the external environment. It also acts as a heat exchanger. It ensures that that fluids, particularly tea and coffee, which are often drunk very hot, are really cool when they arrive in the stomach. The oesophagus, therefore, is obviously much more than a simple connecting tube between the mouth and the stomach.

At the junction of the gullet and stomach is a sphincter or muscular valve. This closes when food enters the stomach and prevents the stomach's acidic contents from washing back into the oesophagus and irritating its lining. However, this mechanism may develop faults as a person ages or gains weight. Pregnancy can affect it and so can heavy lifting.

Known as gastro-oesophageal reflux disease (GORD), this is the commonest type of indigestion in the world and affects about 30 per cent of the population in the West at some time or another. The symptoms are heartburn, belching and, sometimes, painful and difficult swallowing.

How is this relevant to cancer of the gullet? The reflux or flowing back of stomach contents can damage the cells that line the oesophagus by leading to acid irritation and inflammation called oesophagitis. In about 10 percent of GORD sufferers, the gullet's lining cells eventually undergo a change, which leads to the condition called Barrett's Metaplasia. This is not cancer, but is a condition that can lead to cancer.

Cancer of the oesophagus develops from the cells that line it, and it can develop at any point along the length of the gullet. There are two types of oesophageal cancer. The first derives directly from the cells normally lining the gullet, the stratified squamous epithelium. This cancer is called squamous cell carcinoma and, at one time, it was the commonest cancer of the gullet. The second type, adenocarcinoma of the oesophagus, arises from the cells which line the lower oesophagus and results from many years of GORD and Barrett's Metaplasia. These patients often, but not always, also have a hiatus hernia, a condition in which the stomach protrudes through the oesophageal opening.

Once cancer of the oesophagus has actually developed, it spreads in three ways: by direct invasion of the gullet wall, by lymphatics to the lymph nodes and via the blood vessels to distant sites elsewhere in the body. It can spread by all three routes at the same time. Often, the cancer is already in the lymph nodes when a doctor first sees the patient. It is vital to diagnose such cancer as early as possible because a patient's chances of survival depend on the stage the disease has reached, as well as on his or her age.

Cancers of the oesophagus in England and Wales occur in about 14 males and 9.2 females per 100,000 of the population. Between eight and 30 per cent of these patients are likely to survive for five years after diagnosis. Worldwide, about two-thirds of all cases are men, although relatively more males are affected in the UK.

Whether a person is likely to develop the disease seems to depend partly on where they live and what they eat. There are three times as many cases in France as there are in Spain. And within France itself, Burgundy and Normandy have 30 cases per 100,000 compared to the national average of 10 per 100,000 of the population. High incidence figures are seen in China in the Linxian county, where 151 cases per 100,000 males occur and 115 cases per 100,000 females. Even higher rates occur in Iran. There, paradoxically, women are more prone than men. There are 195 cases per 100,000 females and 165 cases per 100,000 males. In both South Africa and in the United States the incidence in black populations has been rising for both sexes. However in white males there is now more adenocarcinoma than squamous cell carcinoma. Adenocarcinoma increased by an astonishing 350 per cent in the 20 years between 1974 and 1994.

In England and Wales, about 7,000 people die each year from cancer of the oesophagus. Relative to the size of the population, there are more cases in Scotland. Increases in this cancer have also been seen in Norway, Sweden and elsewhere in the West.

What puts a person at risk of oesophageal cancer? First, age. Most cases occur in men over the age of 70. The effect of age itself, especially in men, is very striking. For example, only one case per 100,000 population can be expected in those under the age of 40. Among men between 45 and 54 years old, there are 20 cases per 100,000. 155 cases per 100,000 occur in over-55s. That makes John Thaw, aged 60 when he died, part of a sad statistic.

Second, smoking and alcohol consumption. In the West, and especially in northern France, studies have shown that squamous cell carcinoma is strongly related to both smoking and alcohol consumption. Spirit consumption is thought to be more unfavourable than wine drinking. In a French study, in non-smokers who were fairly heavy drinkers – consuming more than 57 units of alcohol per week – the risk of developing oesophageal cancer was 5.1 times the risk for non-smokers who drank much less than this. In those who smoked 20 or more cigarettes per day, but did not drink excessively, the relative risk of developing oesophageal cancer was 18 times that expected in a normal population. When the researchers studied a group who were in the highest categories for both alcohol and tobacco consumption, the relative lifetime risk jumped to 44.4 times the average risk for the non-smoking population who drank moderately.

Other reports from the United States, South Africa, China and Hong Kong have confirmed a relationship between cancer of the oesophagus and smoking and alcohol, with the risk substantially increased for those who over-indulge in both. Heavy users of pipes, hand-rolled and high-tar cigarettes are at the greatest risk among the smokers. However, the disease can also occur in non-smokers and non-drinkers and so this is not the whole story. John Thaw, as various contributors to this book make clear, was once a heavy smoker but he seems to have been only a moderate drinker.

Diet is a key factor, too. It has long been known that the risks of developing both oesophageal and gastric cancers are usually, but not always lower in those who eat more fruit and vegetables.

How do doctors spot it? Most patients with oesophageal cancer complain of difficulty in swallowing. Sometimes food sticks in the gullet, a condition known as dysphagia. This is an 'alarm symptom', demanding urgent investigation. However, some patients with cancer have no swallowing problems. They might just have common symptoms of heartburn, dyspepsia, some lower oesophageal pain or chest discomfort and sometimes nausea and vomiting or weight loss and anaemia.

None of these symptoms is, of course, exclusive to cancer of the oesophagus. For example, up to ten per cent of adults experience heartburn daily and as many as 20 per cent have some of the listed symptoms. It is the *recent* onset of such symptoms in those over the age of 55 that should trigger prompt investigation. It is difficult, though, for the general practitioner to choose who to investigate when so many of his or her patients will have mild or moderate symptoms, yet few (less than two per cent) will turn out to have cancer. Nowadays, the Department of Health Guidelines available on http://www.doh.gov.uk/cancer identify groups of patients who should have 'fast track' investigations within two weeks by rapid access to consultation and investigations.

What tests are used in diagnosis? The gold standard is biopsy. This involves an out-patient procedure in which a slender instrument, called an endoscope, is passed into the gullet using a pain-relieving throat spray while the patient is sedated. The operator can inspect the gullet and can take tissue samples for examination afterwards. It results in a definitive diagnosis of cancer in between 95 and 100 per cent of cases.

There is still a place in the assessment and diagnosis of oesophageal cancer for an X-ray examination before which the patient has swallowed barium, although most specialists no longer consider it as a first-choice investigation. It is useful if a patient has obstruction in the gullet so that the endoscope cannot pass through the narrowed area. The X-ray will measure the length, extent and show fine details of irregularity in the lining of the oesophagus.

Once the cancer has been diagnosed and its spread assessed, the next question is how to treat it. If early polypoidal cancer of the oesophagus is diagnosed and it is confined to the mucous lining, then occasionally it can be removed by snaring the very small tumour using an endoscope. This can have good results in elderly, unfit patients. Most cases, however, are too advanced for this new technique.

At present only about 25–35 per cent of all patients with oesophageal cancer in the United Kingdom are offered surgery, fewer than in several other countries. This is usually because when the specialist first meets the patient, the disease is too advanced and is beyond surgical removal. Nevertheless, surgery is the only treatment that has been shown to offer a chance of prolonged survival. Surgery for oesophageal cancer is best conducted in specialised Cancer Units and Cancer Centres. If the disease is early and confined to the mucous lining of the gullet, five-year survivals of over 80 per cent can be achieved for both forms of oesophageal cancer. The general health and lifestyle of the patient and the experience of the surgeon and anaesthetist with the specialist techniques involved all affect the outcome.

There are various ways of operating on cancer of the oesophagus, but, essentially, one side of the chest is opened and one lung collapsed to allow access to the gullet. A gentle, careful technique and good control of bleeding are essential. The usual method is to fashion the stomach into a gastric tube with which to replace the oesophagus. The aim of the surgery is to remove the cancer and all associated involved lymph nodes completely. This is often a difficult task surgically as, in some cases, nodes in both the chest and abdomen may be involved.

Surgery can complicate things too. Fluid balance problems can render the patient too dry or too wet, with the risk of heart or lung failure. The patient needs to be out of bed as soon as possible afterwards in order to avoid blood clots and deep vein thrombosis. Compression stockings, like those recommended for passengers on long-haul flights, and subcutaneous low-dose heparin injections are important too. Pain, poor respiratory excursion – the inability to take deep breaths –, and lung collapse can all lead to pneumonia and respiratory failure. So the patient needs to be in a high-dependency or special care unit after the operation.

Chemotherapy and radiotherapy have become very much more common in the last ten years. Evidence of their effectiveness has come from European and North American centres. The United Kingdom has been relatively slow to adopt such strategies. They are now much more widely used in Britain, although they don't yet seem to be having much impact on survival rates. Such therapies are sometimes used before surgery and sometimes after it. In some cases they are used independently of surgery.

Even if there is little or nothing that doctors can do to stop the spread of the disease, its symptoms can be treated. This is called palliative treatment. Most patients with oesophageal cancer will receive palliative treatment to relieve swallowing difficulties. As well as chemotherapy and radiotherapy, some patients receive another kind of radiotherapy called Brachytherapy. Other techniques include stents – tubes which expand to keep a malignant stricture open – laser treatment, argon beam treatment, alcohol injection, photodynamic therapy and stretching the oesaphagus. It is important to find a quick way to restore the patient's ability to swallow, but he or she needs treatment with minimum disruption and side effects because life span is often short following palliative measures.

There have been several small-scale trials using new drugs. These have sometimes brought 48–70 per cent short-term relief of symptoms. More, large-scale trials are urgently needed in the assessment of treatment for these advanced cases.

Palliative radiotherapy can improve dysphagia – food sticking in the gullet – for a while, but some patients' quality of life can be improved more rapidly by inserting an expanding metal stent into the gullet. Wall-stents seem to produce fewer complications, although most stented patients can no longer eat normal solid foods and have to rely on liquid or semi-liquid diets for the rest of their lives.

Simple oesophageal dilatation – stretching – will improve 50–70 per cent of patients temporarily. Benefit can last from about ten days up to four weeks, but most clinician's reserve repeated treatment as a last resort for patients nearing death.

Other treatments include absolute alcohol injection, Argon Beam therapy, Neodymium Yag laser treatment and photodynamic therapy using photo sensitisors. All have their enthusiasts, but no satisfactory studies have been done and the benefits are short lived. Many of these methods can be combined in the management of an individual patient with those described above.

Community care and follow-up of oesophageal cancer patients are vital and need further developing in the UK. A patient needs goals to help him or her improve the quality of life. It is important to improve a sufferer's nutrition, attend to specific dietary and bowel needs, provide psycho-social support and alleviate pain and nausea. Good general care is essential too. A hospice, where the patient can rest and often be more comfortable than she or he is in a hospital ward – or even at home – is sometimes the best option.

These aspects of care are the responsibility of special members of a multi-disciplinary cancer team. This includes the palliative care specialists, community cancer nurse specialist and the general practitioner. As well as meeting the needs of individuals, follow-up care is also a form of research through which professionals can devise better ways of helping future sufferers.